Behavior and Development in Fragile X Syndrome

D0931762

Developmental Clinical Psychology and Psychiatry Series

Series Editor: Alan E. Kazdin, Yale University

Recent volumes in this series . . .

Behavior and Development in Fragile X Syndrome

Elisabeth M. Dykens
Robert M. Hodapp
James F. Leckman

Volume 28.
Developmental Clinical Psychology and Psychiatry

SAGE Publications
International Educational and Professional Publisher
Thousand Oaks   London   New Delhi

For information address:

SAGE Publications, Inc.
2455 Teller Road
Thousand Oaks, California 91320

SAGE Publications Ltd.
6 Bonhill Street
London EC2A 4PU
United Kingdom

SAGE Publications India Pvt. Ltd.
M-32 Market
Greater Kailash I
New Delhi 110 048 India

Printed in the United States of America

Library of Congress Cataloging-in-Publication Data

Dykens, Elisabeth M.
    Behavior and development in fragile X syndrome / Elisabeth
M. Dykens, Robert M. Hodapp, James F. Leckman.
        p. cm. — (Developmental clinical psychology and psychiatry ;
v. 28)
    Includes bibliographical references and index.
    ISBN 0-8039-4887-5 (cl). — ISBN 0-8039-4888-3 (pb)
    1. Fragile X syndrome. I. Hodapp, Robert M. II. Leckman, James
F. III. Title. IV. Series.
    [DNLM: 1. Fragile X Syndrome. 2. Fragile X Syndrome—psychology.
W1 DE997NC v. 28   1993 / QS 677 D996d   1994]
RJ506.F73D95   1994
155.45′2—dc20
DNLM/DLC
for Library of Congress   93-31372

94 95 96 10 9 8 7 6 5 4 3 2 1

Sage Production Editor: Astrid Virding

To persons with fragile X syndrome
and their families

CONTENTS

SERIES EDITOR'S INTRODUCTION

Interest in child development and adjustment is by no means new. Yet, only recently has the study of children benefited from advances in both clinical and scientific research. Advances in the social and biological sciences, the emergence of disciplines and subdisciplines that focus exclusively on childhood and adolescence, and greater appreciation of the impact of such influences as the family, peers, and school have helped accelerate research on developmental psychopathology. Apart from interest in the study of child development and adjustment for its own sake, the need to address clinical problems naturally draws one to investigate precursors in childhood and adolescence.

Within a relatively brief period, the study of psychopathology among children and adolescents has proliferated considerably. Several different professional journals, annual book series, and handbooks devoted entirely to the study of children and adolescents and their adjustment document the proliferation of work in the field. Nevertheless, there is a paucity of resource material that presents information in an authoritative, systematic, and disseminable fashion. There is a need within the field to convey the latest developments and to represent different disciplines, approaches, and conceptual views to the topics of childhood and adolescent adjustment and maladjustment.

The Sage Series on **Developmental Clinical Psychology and Psychiatry** is designed to serve uniquely several needs of the field. The series encompasses individual monographs prepared by experts in the fields of clinical child psychology, child psychiatry, child development, and related disciplines. The primary focus is on developmental psychopathology, which refers broadly here to the diagnosis, assessment, treatment, and prevention of problems that arise in the period from infancy through adolescence. A working assumption of the series is that understanding, identifying, and treating problems of youth must draw on multiple disciplines and diverse views within a given discipline.

The task for individual contributors is to present the latest theory and research on various topics including specific types of dysfunction, diagnostic and treatment approaches, and special problem areas that affect adjustment. Core topics within clinical work are addressed by the Series. Authors are asked to bridge potential theory, research, and clinical practice, and to outline the current status and future directions. The goals of the Series and the tasks presented to individual contributors are demanding. We have been extremely fortunate in recruiting leaders in the fields who have been able to translate their recognized scholarship and expertise into highly readable works on contemporary topics.

The topic of the present book is fragile X syndrome, the most common hereditary cause of mental retardation. The disorder is of keen interest in its own right given the personal, clinical, and research issues the disorder raises. In addition, research on the genetics of the disorder has raised the prospect of interesting advances that might pertain to other disorders as well. In the present book, Elisabeth M. Dykens, Robert M. Hodapp, and James F. Leckman examine fragile X in detail. They examine the nature and prevalence of the disorder and significant current advances that resolve and raise questions about the disorder and its expression, and a variety of characteristics of individuals and families with fragile X. Critical issues related to the disorder are detailed, including comorbid conditions, adaptive functioning, speech, language, and other characteristics. In addition, broad clinical/social issues are raised in relation to treatment, prevention, and family counseling. The book is very clearly written, authoritative, and thought provoking.

—*Alan E. Kazdin, Ph.D.*

PREFACE

The motivation for writing this book has come from three groups of people. The first group includes the many professionals—teachers, psychologists, physicians, social workers, and others—who have responded to our research on fragile X syndrome with the well-meaning question "What's fragile X syndrome?" The second group includes both lay people and professionals whose curiosity about fragile X syndrome has been piqued by media depictions of the recent discovery of the fragile X gene. These individuals, however, often lack additional information about the syndrome. The third group of people includes families who are affected by fragile X syndrome. These families have often expressed strong desires to know more about fragile X syndrome, but have had understandable difficulties wading through scientific articles or books aimed at highly specialized, professional audiences.

It is our hope that *Behavior and Development in Fragile X Syndrome* translates scientific findings into a readable format for both parents and professionals. This book thus aims to fill the information gap about fragile X syndrome that has been pointed out to us by well-meaning professionals, curious lay people, and concerned parents. In filling this gap, we provide a succinct overview of the salient features of fragile X syndrome. These features include the prevalence and historical roots of fragile X syndrome; recent genetic discoveries; the wide range of cognitive, linguistic, adaptive, and maladaptive behavior that is found in this syndrome; and recommendations for intervention and treatment.

This book would not have been possible without the continued support of the John Merck Fund and the help of many families who have participated in the Fragile X Syndrome Clinic at the Yale Child Study Center. We would like to thank all of these families for their patience with us and for the knowledge and inspiration that they have provided us over the years.

Our research also would not have been possible without the pivotal help of Sharon Ort, who has shown steadfast dedication to the well-being of so many fragile X boys and their families. We would also like to thank Naomi Azrieli for her sensitive and helpful feedback, and Joel Bregman, Wendy Marans, Rhea Paul, Pat Murphy, Mike Watson, and research assistants David Walker and Davida Zelinsky for their previous and current contributions to our fragile X syndrome research group. Our work has also been facilitated by the support and guidance of Roy Breg, Ed Zigler, and Donald Cohen. Many others have provided us with feedback and encouragement both with this book and with our research on fragile X syndrome in general, including our respective families, friends, and colleagues at RiverView Hospital, and Theodore Fallon, Victoria Seitz, Michael Faulkner, Maren Jones, Amy Dykens, David Evans, Brenda Finucane, and Marvin Rosen. To each of these people, especially to the families of persons with fragile X syndrome to whom we dedicate this book, we offer our thanks.

1

INTRODUCTION: CASE STORY

Patricia Bell was excited about her new job as a health aid at a local senior center. Not only did she like the work, she thought it might also help her get into nursing school. Influenced by her mother, a pediatric nurse, nurse's training had been Patricia's goal since high school, and it was something that she and Scott had agreed to save up for even before they were married.

Eighteen months after she finished nursing school and had returned to work as a nurse at the senior center, Patricia and Scott's son, Jason, was born after a planned, uneventful pregnancy. Anxious and excited about their first child, Patricia had followed her doctor's guidelines for prenatal care meticulously, and she and Scott had attended childbirth classes. There were no complications with the delivery, and 7-pound 14-ounce Jason and his mother were sent home with standard instructions for baby care.

Jason was a healthy infant, although he seemed to have some trouble drinking from his bottle. At times, he also seemed irritable and difficult to soothe, especially at night. At the pediatrician's suggestion, Patricia changed Jason's formula and nap schedule, but these changes did not make him less irritable.

Throughout the next 24 months, Jason remained a finicky child, which Scott thought might be because his wife was spoiling Jason with too much attention. Scott therefore proposed that Patricia return to work part time and that they hire a sitter.

Although Patricia missed her job, she was clearly reluctant to return to work. Patricia worried that a sitter would not know how to handle Jason's irritability and his unpredictable responses to being held. She was reassured, however, by the pediatrician's feedback that some babies, especially boys, were just more "high-strung" than others. Moreover, the

1

pediatrician suggested that Patricia's anxiety as a new parent might be contributing to her son's irritability, and she offered specific ways that mother and son might relax together. Scott and Patricia's family disagreed with the pediatrician. They considered Patricia to be a competent and patient mother; if anything, she was too devoted to her son. Despite Patricia's attentiveness, however, Jason did not seem to be doing well developmentally. He did not have the usual baby talk, he occasionally flapped his hands when excited, and he sometimes seemed in a world of his own.

Patricia's mother was convinced that Jason had allergies that explained his picky eating, overactivity, and resistance to being held. Patricia's sister Valerie, however, felt that Jason acted like an autistic child that she had once seen in a TV movie. She gently tried to tell Patricia about this by pointing out to her how Jason's behavior was different from that of her own two preschoolers. Although Patricia acknowledged some of these differences, she secretly felt that Valerie exaggerated how advanced her own children were to show off that she was the smarter of the two sisters.

By the time Jason was 2½ Scott knew that something was wrong with his son: He hadn't "outgrown" his irritability, and both he and Patricia were often baffled by their son's behaviors. Scott wanted answers from the experts, and with the help of Jason's pediatrician, Patricia and Scott arranged for Jason to be seen in a developmental clinic at a local Children's Hospital.

The intake pediatrician at the Children's Hospital observed that Jason was an active toddler who tolerated the physical exam by sitting briefly on his parents' laps before squirming out of their arms. He was an attractive boy, with blonde hair and hazel eyes, who also seemed to have a large head and rather prominent ears. The doctor further noted that Jason was quite wary and avoidant of eye contact with her, yet he readily sought out his parents and made eye contact with them. He often took his parents' hands and placed them on what he wanted, making limited verbalizations as he did so. As Jason became tired toward the end of the interview, he "played" by flapping his hands next to his ears, humming, and spinning objects.

At the end of the intake, Jason was scheduled to meet with a psychologist for a developmental evaluation. He separated from his parents after considerable protest. The intake pediatrician was then joined by a genetic counselor and a child psychiatrist, who collectively took a history of

Jason, and also a detailed history of Patricia and Scott and their extended families.

Both Scott and Patricia were physically healthy, as were most members of their extended families. Similarly, their extended families did not have significant psychological problems. Patricia, who was becoming increasingly put off by these lengthy and personal questions, decided not to tell the doctors about her occasional struggles with math in both high school and nurses training. She did tell them, however, that she had a maternal uncle with psychological problems.

Upon further questioning about her uncle, Patricia offered that Uncle Ron was a slow learner who had spent his school years with her aunt's family on their dairy farm. He helped with farming chores, and after the farm was sold, he went to live in a group home for persons with mental retardation. Uncle Ron was now in his late 50s, and was physically healthy.

By this point in the interview, both Patricia and Scott began to feel that the doctors had forgotten about Jason altogether. Patricia was annoyed enough to interrupt and ask just exactly what her uncle had to do with Jason's problems. She was told that Jason seemed to have certain delays and atypical, autistic-like features of his development that warranted further tests. Some of these tests could establish whether Jason had a genetic disorder that may have been passed through her family. Patricia later told Scott that she was so devastated by these words that she could hardly listen to what else the team said to them that day.

Scott, however, listened attentively, and later re-explained to his wife that the doctors did not know yet if Jason was autistic, and that he might have a genetic disorder called fragile X syndrome. They wanted to observe Jason again and also to test him for fragile X syndrome by looking at the DNA in his blood. In order to find out who had the syndrome, the team also wanted to test Patricia's blood, as well as blood from her mother, father, sister, nephews, and others in the family. Although they could also test Scott's blood, they thought that if the syndrome was present, it probably began years ago with one of Patricia's distant relatives, even before her maternal grandmother might have passed it on to her Uncle Ron.

For Patricia, the next few weeks passed in a blur. Jason's blood was drawn, and he was videotaped playing with her and Scott. The psychologist recommended a special preschool program at the hospital, and Patricia spent several mornings enrolling Jason in the program and observing how he did with the other students. Patricia, her sister Valerie, and her mother and father all had their blood drawn, and arrangements were also made for Uncle Ron's blood to be drawn.

When the day of their family conference with the hospital team arrived, Patricia knew what the results of the tests were even before they walked into the clinic. Jason had tested positive for fragile X syndrome, and so had Patricia. They also learned that Uncle Ron and Patricia's mother had tested positive; Valerie's test was negative.

The counselors emphasized that people cannot change their genes, there was no control over the situation, they were not responsible for their DNA, and that Patricia and Scott had clearly done everything that was within their control to ensure that Jason was a healthy child. These reassurances did not stop the waves of guilt and self-blame that Patricia suddenly felt. When the doctors used words like *mutation* and *carrier* it confirmed for Patricia that her genes were somehow damaged and had caused her son to be damaged. She was too upset to listen further, and questions raced through Patricia's mind. What did it mean that she had a "mutation"? Why did she and her mother have this gene and not Valerie? What could they expect of Jason? What about future children? And what was this fragile X syndrome, anyhow? No one in her or Scott's family had ever heard of it before.

The story of Patricia, Scott, and Jason is a common one. Indeed, fragile X syndrome may be the most prevalent inherited genetic disorder in the population to date (Sherman, 1992; Warren, 1992). As an X-linked syndrome that generally results in mental retardation and characteristic physical and behavioral features, fragile X syndrome affects immediate and extended family members of several generations.

This introductory chapter describes the prevalence and historical roots of fragile X syndrome, while the remainder of the book is devoted to the behavioral characteristics of this disorder. Specifically, many features suggested by the story of Patricia, Scott, and Jason will be described, including the physical characteristics of Jason and other affected males and females; the links between fragile X syndrome and Jason's autistic behaviors and apparent hyperactivity; Patricia's occasional struggles with math; her self-blame upon learning of the diagnosis; and how Patricia, her mother, and Uncle Ron could be affected with fragile X but not her sister Valerie. Other questions raised by Patricia will also be addressed—her concerns about having other children, as well as her uncertainties about Jason's course of development.

PREVALENCE OF FRAGILE X SYNDROME

Although many kinds of mental retardation are linked to the X chromosome, fragile X syndrome may account for 30% to 50% of all of these cases (Herbst & Miller, 1980; Webb, 1989). Fragile X syndrome has been found—in approximately equal frequencies—in every ethnic group in which it has been studied, including most European countries, as well as countries in Africa, Central and South America, India, and the Orient (see Webb, 1989, for a review). Researchers have estimated that fragile X syndrome affects as many as 1 in 750 to 1,000 males and 1 in 500 to 750 females (e.g., Gustavson, Blomquist, & Holgren, 1986; Opitz, 1986, 1987; Sherman, 1992).

These prevalence figures are second only to Down syndrome in terms of a known, genetic cause of mental retardation. Down syndrome, however, is not inherited from one generation to another; instead, the genetic anomalies occur in the reproductive cells of the mother. In contrast, fragile X syndrome is passed on through families. As such, fragile X syndrome is the most common *hereditary* cause of mental retardation.

Although a common disorder, most cases of fragile X syndrome have yet to be identified, making unclear the exact prevalence of this disorder (Warren, 1992). So many unidentified cases are due, in part, to genetic peculiarities of this syndrome that have long baffled geneticists. As discussed in Chapter 2, these peculiarities include a genetic "pre-mutation" or vulnerability that amplifies in size as it is passed down through generations of families until it reaches a "full mutation"—an individual who is fully affected with the fragile X syndrome. The prevalence of these pre-mutations in the general population remains unknown, as does the length of time that it takes for pre-mutations to progress to full mutations (Shapiro, 1991).

These unique genetic characteristics become even more puzzling in that approximately one third to one half of the females who carry and transmit fragile X are actually affected with a variant of the syndrome themselves. Many of these "carrier females" show varying degrees of learning difficulties as well as vulnerabilities toward certain emotional problems. Rarely, some of these females are more seriously impaired with mild to moderate mental retardation. Approximately one half of carrier females, however, are unaffected by fragile X syndrome, yet may still transmit the disorder to their offspring.

Males with fragile X syndrome also have an odd genetic twist that further complicates prevalence estimates. Specifically, although most males with fragile X syndrome are mentally retarded, approximately one-fifth are of average intelligence. These so called "non-penetrant" males are unaffected with fragile X syndrome, yet necessarily transmit the vulnerability to their daughters, who, in turn become carriers.

These unique genetic features, discussed more fully in Chapter 2, have meant that researchers have had to extrapolate the population prevalence of fragile X syndrome from studies using mentally retarded samples. Although these studies generally concur that about 1 in 1,000 males and 1 in 750 females are affected, the frequency of identified fragile X cases is likely to increase due to the discovery of the fragile X *FMR-1* gene, and more precise detection of the disorder at the molecular level (Warren, 1992).

THE HISTORY OF
FRAGILE X SYNDROME

The puzzling and unusual genetic features of fragile X syndrome have challenged many classical and traditional ideas in genetics and in the field of mental retardation. But to appreciate these challenges fully, as well as current genetic breakthroughs, requires some brief historical background.

Throughout the 20th century, researchers have postulated what has been called the "two-group" approach in the field of mental retardation (Zigler, 1967). Promoted especially by Zigler and his colleagues beginning in the late 1960s, the two-group approach states that there are two types of mental retardation: organic mental retardation and familial or cultural-familial mental retardation. Persons with the first type show a clear organic cause of their retardation due to insults occurring prenatally (e.g., all genetic disorders), perinatally (e.g., anoxia at birth), or postnatally (e.g., meningitis, head trauma). Organic retardation accounts for somewhat less than half of all persons with mental retardation (Zigler & Hodapp, 1986a).

The second category involves persons who show no clear organic cause for their mental retardation. This group has been called by a variety of names: familial, cultural-familial, or sociocultural retardation; nonorganic mental retardation; and idiopathic retardation. These individuals are generally mildly retarded, often have one or more family members who are also retarded, and are much more likely to be minorities and of a low socioeconomic status. Theories as to the cause of their retardation range from genetic to environmental; indeed, to this day, many consider poor environments to be the primary cause of this type of mental retardation. In genetics as well, many basic laws were formulated in the period before about 1960. Only in the late 1950s did it become clear that humans have 23 pairs of chromosomes, and that Down syndrome is caused by the addition of a third chromosome 21. Cytogenetic testing, a technique for making chromosomes visible under the microscope, was also developed and refined at about this time.

THE DISCOVERY OF FRAGILE X SYNDROME

In 1943, Martin and Bell published a pedigree of what appeared to be X-linked mental retardation, where sons and uncles were affected, with no father-to-son transmission, and sparing of females. By the early 1960s, several other families with this type of transmission had been reported by several research groups (e.g., Dunn, Renpenning, & Gerrard, 1963; Opitz, Segal, Klove, Mathews, & Lehrke, 1965).

The idea of a major, X-linked form of mental retardation was originally greeted with skepticism by many workers in mental retardation. This skepticism is best shown by the story of Robert Lehrke. Lehrke, a graduate student in education at the University of Wisconsin, performed a major study of X-linked mental retardation for his dissertation. Lehrke's (1974) study noted that males have always been overrepresented in surveys of persons with retardation, in either institutional or community settings. He further noted that in families with more than one child with mental retardation, more male-male sibling pairs were found than male-female or female-female pairs. After reviewing what appeared to be X-linked mental retardation in many families, Lehrke concluded that genes on the X chromosome were responsible for a large percentage of persons with mental retardation.

Although Lehrke was considered "a prescient genius" whose dissertation is "a classic in the field" (Opitz, 1986), his ideas initially received a less-than-enthusiastic reception, especially from behaviorally oriented workers in mental retardation. As Lehrke's mentor Opitz (1986) recalls, "The psychology members of the [dissertation] committee were so appalled by the genetic implications of Lehrke's studies and conclusions that they begged him to tone down this aspect of his thesis; it was only after acceding to their request that he . . . was awarded his degree" (p. 3). Lehrke's (1972) paper in the *American Journal of Mental Deficiency* (*AJMD*) was also greeted skeptically (Anastasi, 1972). Two forces were acting against the acceptance of Lehrke's ideas. The first was the Zeitgeist of the times. For the most part, the 1960s were a period in which environmental, as opposed to genetic, explanations for behavior and development dominated. Scarr and Weinberg (1978) have characterized the period as one of "naive environmentalism," a time during which there were strong, almost mystical beliefs in the power of the environment to determine intelligence, and genetic factors were de-emphasized. The second problem was that no cytogenetic evidence was yet available for fragile X syndrome. Even Lubs's (1969) discovery of the fragile site on the long arm of the X chromosome (that looked pinched off and constricted, hence the name "fragile") was problematic in that his finding could not be replicated. Indeed, in Lubs's original report, the cognitive and behavioral problems of the two affected siblings were attributed to environmental factors in the family. As late as the mid-1970s, some geneticists were finding this fragile site (e.g., Harvey, Judge, & Weiner, 1976), while others were not, and no one knew quite how to explain the discrepancies. Only in 1977 did Sutherland resolve this issue by noting that the fragile site on the X chromosome is only seen when cytogenetic testing is performed using a medium that is deficient in folate (see Chapter 2).

Since the 1970s, there have been major advances in the genetics of fragile X syndrome; these advances have lead to more and more persons being diagnosed with this syndrome. Increasing numbers of fragile X cases have important implications for the two-group approach. Specifically, Dykens and Leckman (1990) note that the definition of familial retardation is consistent with many cases of fragile X syndrome: both "run in families" (Zigler & Hodapp, 1986a, p. 51), involve a mildly impaired parent, and possibly, affected siblings. Many of these familial-cultural cases may test positive for fragile X syndrome, thereby increasing the percentages of persons considered to have organic mental retardation.

Indeed, studies of groups with cultural-familial mental retardation show that at least some of these individuals have fragile X syndrome. Thake, Todd, Webb, and Bundey (1987) screened nonorganic, mildly retarded school boys in England and found that 8% of these boys actually had fragile X syndrome. Similarly, Bundey, Webb, Thake, and Todd (1985) found that 9% of severely impaired boys described as having idiopathic retardation tested positive for fragile X syndrome. Other studies have screened institutionalized, idiopathic mentally retarded men and found rates of fragile X syndrome that ranged from approximately 2% (Sutherland, 1982) to 11% (Turner, Robinson, Laing, & Purvis-Smith, 1986). These studies suggest that, at present, as many as 10% of males now classified as having nonorganic mental retardation may have fragile X syndrome, regardless of impairment or institutional status. Furthermore, these percentages are likely to increase as new cases are identified with more accurate molecular testing. Although fragile X syndrome does not invalidate the two-group idea, it does markedly change the percentages in each group.

PLAN OF THE BOOK

Fragile X syndrome is the most common inherited disorder in the population to date, manifested not only in mental retardation, but also in a wide spectrum of learning and emotional problems in both males and females. The impact of this disorder on the general population is thus far-reaching, extending beyond mentally retarded males to include many as yet undetected individuals who fall in this spectrum of learning and emotional problems.

Many people in the general population, however, remain unaware of this baffling syndrome. This is primarily because information about fragile X syndrome has remained largely in genetic and biomedical journals, where it is less accessible to the public, as well as to families, special educators, social workers, psychologists, mental health and mental retardation workers, and others who provide care for affected individuals and their families. The goal of this book is to fill in this information gap.

Consistent with this aim, Chapter 2 describes the many genetic peculiarities of fragile X syndrome. It reviews the recent discovery of the fragile X *FMR-1* gene, and includes some terms and concepts that may be challenging for readers without a background in biology. Some readers may choose to skim this section and to focus instead on the issues of genetic screening and counseling that are presented at the end of the chapter.

Chapter 3 summarizes the physical features of both males and females with fragile X syndrome, and describes how many of these unusual features change with development.

Chapters 4, 5, and 6 describe intellectual, linguistic, and adaptive functioning, respectively. In each of these chapters, characteristic strengths and weaknesses are discussed, as are whether these profiles are unique to fragile X syndrome or found in other groups of mentally retarded persons. These chapters also present information on the trajectory and rate of development, and similarities and differences in the functioning of fragile X males versus females.

Chapter 7 discusses psychopathology and maladaptive behavior in fragile X syndrome. Particular attention is given to the autism controversy, social relatedness issues, and hyperactivity and attention deficits. Less common psychiatric disorders in males are also presented, as is the growing literature on psychopathology among carrier females.

Chapter 8 reviews various recommendations for intervention and treatment that stem from the behavioral profiles and maladaptive features of fragile X syndrome. But before discussing these behavioral issues in fragile X syndrome, we first describe the genetics of this puzzling disorder.

2

GENETIC FACTORS

Fragile X syndrome is the result of an unstable region of genetic material found on the long arm of the X chromosome (Yu et al., 1991). The ability to diagnose this syndrome accurately has evolved over the past two decades from the initial cytogenetic discovery of the fragile X site by Lubs in 1969, to the actual cloning of the fragile X gene by a number of laboratories in Europe and the United States in the early 1990s. The technological advances that are responsible for the identification of the fragile X gene also place us on the threshold of discoveries that will likely lead to innovative strategies for treatment and prevention of this disabling condition. Although a close examination of the genetic basis of this syndrome requires some familiarity with genetic concepts, this knowledge is worthwhile for parents and clinicians because it serves as the basis for the genetic counseling of families.

On the other hand, much of the chapter is fairly technical and may be difficult to follow without some background in biology. In addition, some of the scientific terms used, such as *mutation,* can be upsetting because of the images such words bring to mind. For those readers who decide to skim over this chapter, the essence is simply that one specific gene out of the 100,000 or so genes that all humans have does not work right, and it causes fragile X syndrome.

GENES AND CHROMOSOMES

Our genetic endowment is a unique collection of discrete units of heredity, called genes. Genes are basically biological messages that are transmitted from one generation to the next. Genes are usually linearly arranged on chromosomes that are found in the nuclei of cells. In humans, genes are arranged on 46 chromosomes; 22 different pairs of homologous, or identical, chromosomes called autosomes, and the two sex chromo-

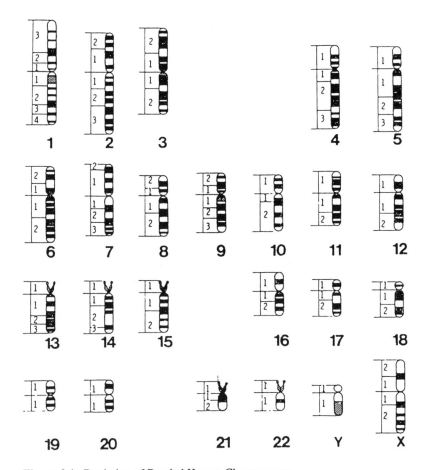

Figure 2.1. Depiction of Banded Human Chromosomes
SOURCE: Adapted from Yale-HHMI Human Gene Mapping Library.

somes, with XX producing a female and XY a male (see Figure 2.1). Normally, genes are extremely stable and are precisely copied during the duplications of chromosomes that precede cell divisions (the processes of mitosis and meiosis).

Gene Structure

Chemically, genes are composed of deoxyribonucleic acid, or DNA. DNA, in turn, is made up of a string of nucleotides that are linked end to end. Nucleotides are complex molecules that contain a sugar, a phosphate group, and a nucleic acid. Four separate nucleotides are found in DNA. Two contain purine bases—either adenine (A) or guanine (G)—and two contain pyrimidine bases—either thymine (T) or cytosine (C). Genetic information is conveyed by the specific ordering of these four A, G, T, and C nucleotides.

DNA is arranged in a specific "double-helix" arrangement. The best way to think of this double-helix arrangement is as a twisted ladder or a spiral staircase, with the sugars and phosphates forming the sides of the ladder, and the base elements forming the "steps." Furthermore, each step is composed of a pair of two base elements. Adenine (A) always binds with thymine (T) and guanine (G) always binds with cytosine (C) (see Figure 2.2). This structure confers stability to the DNA molecule and provides the basis for replication. Because each strand of DNA in the double helix is exactly complementary to the other, knowing the sequence of one strand (or side of the ladder) immediately provides precise information about the sequence of the other strand. The discovery of the double helix of DNA is the essence of the famous work of Watson and Crick, which is summarized in Watson's (1968) very readable book *The Double Helix*.

Gene Function

The sequence of complementary base pairs in DNA determines the order of the 20 different amino acids that make up proteins. As a consequence, the information contained in DNA provides instructions on how to build proteins that, in turn, direct cells to do any number of things—to grow and divide, to set in motion developmental sequences that lead to the differentiation of cell types, and to maintain diverse populations of cells that are necessary for the successful functioning of complex organisms.

The sequence of complementary base pairs in DNA, however, does not provide a direct template for the synthesis of these proteins. Instead, there is a complex series of events that depends on the "transcription" of the genetic code from DNA to a "messenger"—messenger ribonucleic acid, or mRNA. Messenger RNA is very similar in composition to DNA and can bind to complementary DNA sequences. Messenger RNA conveys the information out of the nucleus and into the cytoplasm, or the area of the cell that surrounds the nucleus, and serves as the template for protein synthesis.

After the transcribed RNA leaves the nucleus, the "translation" of the genetic code into a specific amino acid sequence occurs at ribosomes,

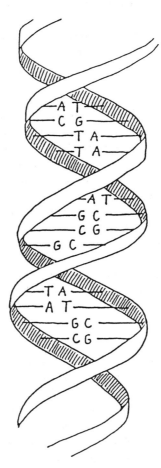

Figure 2.2. A Model of DNA Showing A, G, T, and C Nucleotides in the Double-Helix, "Twisted Ladder" Arrangement

SOURCE: Figure courtesy of Amy Dykens.

structures that the mRNA attach to in the cytoplasm of the cell. The genetic code is determined by the sequence of bases, with sets of three bases constituting one coding unit or "codon." At the ribosome, the codons of an mRNA molecule base-pair with complementary "anticodons" of transfer RNAs, or tRNA. The tRNA contribute specific amino acids to the growing protein chain.

Abnormalities in Gene Structure and Function

Mutations, or heritable changes in the structure of genes, can occur. Frequently, these changes are of no functional consequence. If, however, the change occurs in a site that corresponds to a critically important region of the gene, the effects can be deleterious. In some cases, a poorly functioning or nonfunctioning protein would be formed because of the mutation. In other cases, called *null* mutations, no gene product is formed at all. Fragile X syndrome is usually the result of a null mutation.

Transmission

As noted above, genes serve critical functions for living organisms. They store information in the nuclei of cells; they pass information from the nucleus to the cytoplasm concerning which proteins and enzymes to make; and they pass, or transmit, this information on from one generation to the next.

In order to understand the transmission of genetic material from one generation to the next, it is important to recall that genes are linearly arrayed on chromosomes and that there are 46 human chromosomes divided into 22 different pairs of homologous chromosomes, called autosomes, and one pair of sex chromosomes (see Figure 2.1). The pattern of transmission differs according to whether or not the gene of interest is on one of the 22 autosomes, called "autosomal transmission," or on a sex chromosome, called "Y- or X-linked transmission."

Autosomal Transmission. In one form of autosomal inheritance, *autosomal dominant inheritance,* only one copy of the abnormal gene is required to produce a disease. In autosomal dominant inheritance, there is a 50% chance that any child will inherit the abnormal gene, and males and females are at equal risk. Because only one parent needs to have the abnormal gene for the disease to appear generation after generation, autosomal dominant disorders often appear in multiple generations. Huntington's chorea is one such autosomal dominant disorder.

A second form of autosomal inheritance, *autosomal recessive inheritance,* requires that both parents have at least one abnormal copy of the gene in question because the disease will only appear when a child has two copies of the abnormal gene. In this form of inheritance, in which the abnormal gene is "recessive" to the normal gene, there is only a 25% chance that any child will inherit both of the abnormal genes. However, there is a 75% chance that any child will inherit at least one of the abnormal genes. Cystic fibrosis is an example of an autosomal recessive disorder.

X-Linked Transmission. Recall that females have two X chromosomes (XX) and males only have one X chromosome (XY). This means that mothers can "carry" and pass on an abnormal gene on their X chromosome to either their sons or daughters, but fathers can only pass on an abnormal gene on the X chromosome to their daughters. In X-linked disorders such as color-blindness or hemophilia, "carrier" females and their daughters are perfectly normal because they have a second X chromosome with a normal copy of the gene, thereby "buffering" deleterious effects from the abnormal gene. If, however, a son receives an abnormal copy of the gene from his mother, he usually will be affected because he only has one X chromosome.

Another important feature of X-linked transmission concerns the fact that in any given cell only one X chromosome is active. In boys and men, who only have one X chromosome, that chromosome is always active. In the case of girls and women, who have two X chromosomes, one of their X chromosomes is active and the other is inactive. This process of X inactivation occurs very early in development. The molecular basis of this process is not well understood nor is there a good understanding of the factors, other than chance, that determine which X chromosome remains active and which is inactivated.

THE GENE RESPONSIBLE FOR
FRAGILE X SYNDROME

Structure of the *FMR-1* Gene

Individuals affected with fragile X syndrome have a null mutation of the *FMR-1* gene in which the levels of protein in mRNA *FMR-1* are greatly reduced (Pieretti et al., 1991). Although the structure of this gene has not been fully characterized, it does contain some unusual elements. These elements include a highly repetitive sequence of the bases cytosine-guanine-guanine, or $(CGG)_n$, that appears to lengthen dramatically in affected individuals (Fu et al., 1991).

Analyses of variations in length of the $(CGG)_n$ region in individuals *without* fragile X syndrome show remarkable variation in the number of repeats, from 6 to 54, with 29 repeats being the most frequent number in normal individuals (Fu et al., 1991). Individuals affected with fragile X syndrome have been found to have from 200 to more than 1,000 CGG repeats; these affected individuals are said to have the *full mutation*. The extreme amplification of this CGG repeat sequence is likely to be the fragile X mutation site in the great majority of cases.

Other family members in affected fragile X pedigrees may have numbers of CGG repeats that fall in between normal individuals and those who are fully affected with fragile X syndrome. These family members have CGG repeats that are in an intermediate zone, or between 52 and 200 repeats (Fu et al., 1991). Because this intermediate alteration has not been associated with the full fragile X phenotype, repeats in this range are called *pre-mutations* (Oberlé et al., 1991).

In addition to the 200 to 1,000 CGG repeats in affected fragile X males, there are abnormalities in nearby regions called CpG "islands"; these structures are thought to play a role in gene regulation. These CpG islands are abnormally methylated in affected fragile X males (Oberlé et al., 1991); *methylation* refers to a chemical change in the DNA structure that alters its activity. Methylation at the CpG islands correlates with the loss of expression of the *FMR-1* mRNA (Pieretti et al., 1991). The extreme variations in the CGG repeat sequence in affected fragile X individuals appear to induce methylation, which in turn, down regulate the expression of the *FMR-1* mRNA, ultimately leading to the null mutation seen in fragile X males.

To date, similar genetic mechanisms are known to underlie only three other inherited disorders, including myotonic dystrophy and Huntington's chorea. Myotonic dystrophy involves alterations in the length of a CTG repeat sequence that are responsible for a range of clinical problems including the failure of muscles to relax after forceful contraction, muscle wasting, cardiac arrhythmias, and hormonal problems (e.g., Fu et al., 1992). As in fragile X syndrome, the basis for genetic instability in these CG rich areas remains unclear (Caskey, Pizzuti, Fu, Fenwick, & Nelson, 1992).

It is possible that other abnormalities besides the extreme amplification of the CGG triplet repeat could lead to a null mutation of the *FMR-1* gene. For example, a deletion of a portion of the *FMR-1* gene would result in a null mutation and in a similar or identical clinical presentation to an individual with a full mutation. In potential cases of partial deletions, the DNA tests described below would be negative because they depend on the presence of the triplet repeat. Such cases should be referred to a research laboratory so that a full assessment of the mutation can be made.

Function of the *FMR-1* Gene

Although forms of the *FMR-1* gene have been conserved over the course of evolution (Verkerk et al., 1991), the normal function of the *FMR-1* gene and its protein product are unknown. In humans, the gene is known to be expressed in a variety of tissues, with high levels in the brain and testes. This distribution corresponds to the most consistent and salient features of affected fragile X males—mental retardation, enlargement of the head (slight) and testes (marked). Although the mechanism by which the down regulation of the *FMR-1* gene leads to these features is presently unknown, ongoing research is likely to unravel this mystery in the near future.

Location of the *FMR-1* Gene

As reviewed in Chapter 1, in 1969 Lubs made the initial discovery of a cytogenetic abnormality on the long arm of the X chromosome, called Xq, associated with what is now known as fragile X syndrome. Genetic linkage studies using traditional methods of tracing the vertical descent of portions of chromosomes from one generation to the next within large families localized the mutation to Xq27 (Suthers et al., 1991). The precise physical location and isolation of the *FMR-1* gene was then accomplished using state-of-the-art molecular biological techniques (Warren et al., 1990; Verkerk et al., 1991).

Transmission of the *FMR-1* Gene

Fragile X syndrome is transmitted from one generation to the next as an X-linked disorder. The X-linked transmission of fragile X syndrome, however, is highly unusual for two reasons. First, approximately 20% of the males who carry the abnormal gene are not mentally impaired (Sherman, Morton, Jacobs, & Turner, 1984; Sherman et al., 1985). These men, called "normal transmitting males," can pass the abnormal gene to their daughters who are also usually unaffected. These males' grandsons, however, are often affected with the full syndrome. This progression in severity from one generation to the next is termed "anticipation" by geneticists and has come to be known as the "Sherman paradox" in fragile X syndrome.

Another unusual inheritance feature in fragile X syndrome concerns the clinical status of the carrier females. Unlike other X-linked disorders (such as hemophilia or color-blindness), more than one third of the carrier

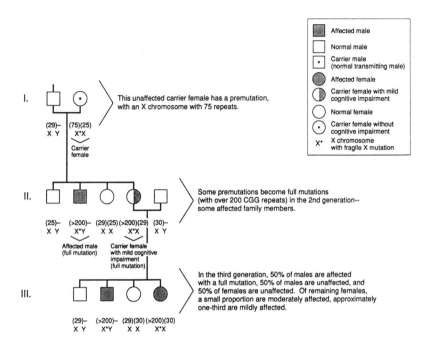

Figure 2.3. Transmission of Fragile X Syndrome Across Three Generations in a Hypothetical Pedigree Beginning With a Non-Affected Carrier Female

NOTE: Numbers in parentheses refer to the number of CGG triplet repeats in the *FMR-1* genes found on each of the X chromosomes: normal X chromosomes have 6 to 50 repeats with most having 29 repeats; pre-mutation X chromosomes have 52 to 200 repeats; and full mutations have > 200 repeats.

females of fragile X syndrome are themselves affected with some degree of mental impairment, although many others are perfectly normal (Sherman et al., 1984; Sherman et al., 1985).

Recent evidence has shown that each of these unusual features can be mostly accounted for by variations in the length of the CGG triplet repeat sequence, and the tendency for pre-mutations to expand to full mutations when they are passed through females but not males (Fu et al., 1991). These phenomena are depicted in Figures 2.3 and 2.4. Figure 2.3 shows three generations from a hypothetical fragile X family pedigree that involves the children and grandchildren of an unaffected carrier female with a "pre-mutation." Figure 2.4 depicts a similar three-generational set from a hypothetical fragile X pedigree beginning with an unaffected non-penetrant male.

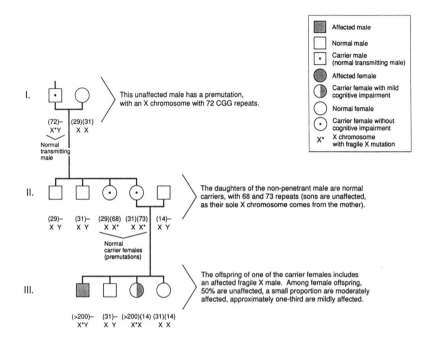

Figure 2.4. Transmission of Fragile X Syndrome Across Three Generations in a Hypothetical Pedigree Beginning With an Unaffected, Non-Penetrant Male

NOTE: Numbers in parentheses refer to the number of triplet repeats in the *FMR-1* genes found on each of the X chromosomes: normal X chromosomes have 6 to 50 repeats with most having 29 repeats; pre-mutation X chromosomes have 52 to 200 repeats; and full mutations have > 200 repeats.

Males and females with pre-mutations (52 to 200 triplet repeats), in the first generation of both pedigrees, do not show cognitive impairments. Amplification of CGG repeats only occurs with either affected or unaffected carrier females in the first pedigree (Table 2.3), and through the normal carrier daughters of the non-penetrant male in the second pedigree (Table 2.4). Although the mechanisms responsible for this amplification when pre-mutations are passed to next generation via the mother are unclear, it has been well established that the risk for expansion to a full mutation increases dramatically once the number of repeats exceeds 70 (Fu et al., 1991).

The phenomenon of X-inactivation (whereby one of the female's X chromosomes is active and the other inactive) probably also plays an important role in determining the range of clinical variation in carrier females. X-inactivation works in such a way that individuals who by chance have fewer affected cell lines in the tissues of the brain (i.e., fewer cells in which the abnormal X chromosome remains active) will be less severely affected.

DIAGNOSIS

Cytogenetic Techniques

The development of cytogenetic techniques reached a level of clinical utility with the discovery that the fragile site at Xq27 could be induced by culturing blood cells in folate-deficient media (Sutherland, 1977). This was an expensive, labor-intensive technique that frequently gave equivocal results, particularly with carrier females and in prenatal diagnosis. With the cytogenetic test, the proportion of X chromosomes showing folate-sensitive fragility was rarely more than 40% to 50% among affected males and 0% to 40% in carrier females. Women who had some degree of cognitive impairment were more likely to show folate-sensitive fragility in 5% or more of the cells examined. Prior to the 1990s, cytogenetic techniques were the only diagnostic tests available. Most individuals known to have fragile X syndrome today were diagnosed with this procedure.

Current Approaches

Advanced molecular genetic techniques are the basis of the current diagnostic approaches to fragile X syndrome. These techniques are less expensive and take less time than cytogenetics, and they also have a high level of accuracy when performed correctly. A sample of blood is needed for these techniques, and DNA is then isolated from the blood cells.

The most common technique, the *Southern blot transfer,* simply looks for the degree of amplification of the length of the *FMR-1* gene. The DNA from the patient's blood is digested with certain enzymes that only work at particular sequence sites that are known to occur in DNA. The DNA fragments are then linearly arrayed in a gel according to their size using an electrophoretic technique. The DNA is then transferred (Southern transfer) to a membrane and probed with a radioactive or fluorescently labeled piece of DNA that only recognizes the *FMR-1* gene. If the piece of DNA from the individual being tested is larger than normal, then a presumptive diagnosis of fragile X syndrome is made. Southern blot techniques can also be used to detect the methylation of the *FMR-1* gene.

Another recently developed molecular technique, called *polymerase chain reaction* or *PCR,* offers the rapid detection of copies (or alleles) of the *FMR-1* gene that are in the normal range, as well as pre-mutation alleles that have 50 to 200 triplet repeats (Caskey et al., 1992). Some investigators have even reported that PCR techniques can be used to detect the full mutation (Pergolizzi, Erster, Goonewardena, & Brown, 1992). These PCR techniques take advantage of our knowledge of the actual nucleotide sequence of the *FMR-1* gene, particularly in those regions that are immediately adjacent to, or flanking, the variable CGG repeat so that special DNA primers can be synthesized. The PCR techniques depend on the use of a heat stable enzyme that makes a new strand of DNA using an existing DNA strand as a template. The patient's DNA is used as a template and is placed together with the special DNA primers and the heat stable DNA polymerase. The reaction mixture is then allowed to cycle through a series of temperature changes that allow thousands of copies of the DNA region between the special primers to be synthesized. The products of this reaction are then linearly arrayed in a gel according to their size using an electrophoretic technique. These results should give a good indication of the size of the triplet repeat. Other techniques that are likely to be developed in the near future include assays or tests for the *FMR-1* protein product, and analyzing genetic polymorphisms that flank the region of DNA instability.

SCREENING FOR
FRAGILE X SYNDROME

As the most common inherited disorder in the general population to date, fragile X syndrome is a major public health problem (Partington, 1988). This public health problem could be addressed by screening programs that test for fragile X syndrome in a variety of different groups. The decision of which groups to screen for fragile X syndrome, however, remains controversial.

Screening At-Risk Groups for
Fragile X Syndrome

Some researchers advocate that *all* developmentally delayed or at-risk individuals receive testing for fragile X syndrome. Hagerman, Amiri, and

Cronister (1991) conclude that "cytogenetic testing should be considered in all individuals with mental retardation of unknown etiology" (p. 286). This approach is optimally sensitive in that it identifies all fragile X cases, yet would necessarily involve testing many individuals who do not have the syndrome.

Others, however, have developed screening instruments that identify mentally retarded persons with a high probability of having fragile X syndrome (e.g., Butler, Mangrum, Gupta, & Singh, 1991). These at-risk males have been identified in school, institutional, and clinic settings based on certain physical and behavioral features often observed in fragile X syndrome.

These physical features, however, will not be as helpful in screening non-penetrant males and carrier females, as these two groups do not generally manifest distinctive physical features or obvious mental retardation. Yet some of these individuals may show subtle neurobehavioral dysfunction; as such, Reiss et al. (1992) have devised a cognitive/behavioral questionnaire that screens for individuals who have these problems within fragile X families.

Screening the General Population for
Fragile X Syndrome

In addition to screening developmentally delayed groups for the fragile X marker, screening programs could also be instituted in the general population. These programs could target any number of groups, including those who are not identified as mentally retarded, such as all newborns, school-age children, special education students, or pregnant women. Although an ambitious undertaking, advances in screening and genetic testing (to identify both full and pre-mutations) have made it more realistic for society to consider large-scale fragile X screening programs for various groups in the general population.

The issue of widespread screening is obviously a difficult public policy issue. As Sherman (1992) notes, widespread screening presents both advantages and disadvantages. Advantages of these screening programs include early intervention with affected individuals, and genetic counseling and more informed choices for families at risk for transmitting the disorder. Widespread screening would also increase public awareness of fragile X syndrome. Disadvantages include possible stigmatization of carriers and affected individuals, occasional errors in genetic tests for full and pre-mutations, and the lack of a specific treatment for fragile X.

Unlike fragile X testing in families, screening and genetic testing of the population at large involves making clinically sensitive decisions at the societal level. As such, Sherman (1992) advocates that education about fragile X syndrome must precede any screening effort in the general population. Until communities are better informed about fragile X and can offer appropriate plans for large-scale screening, it seems reasonable that screening and genetic testing should primarily continue to target carrier females and males who are at risk for transmitting the disorder, as well as developmentally delayed individuals who might have the full fragile X mutation.

GENETIC COUNSELING

Once an initial diagnosis of fragile X syndrome is made within a family, referral to a genetic counseling service is recommended. At these sites, trained counselors can meet with family members to discuss the implications of the diagnosis and to plan with the family what other testing should be done. This counseling usually begins with collecting as much information as possible concerning the size and composition of the family tree (or pedigree), and a determination if there are likely to be other cases or carriers of fragile X syndrome.

Young families in at-risk pedigrees may be in particular need of genetic counseling to assess their risks for having a child with fragile X syndrome. With results from the latest diagnostic tests on parents and other key family members, it is now possible to determine with a high degree of certainty whether a woman is a carrier of a full mutation or a pre-mutation of the *FMR-1* gene. If the mother has a pre-mutation, it is also possible to identify what the risks are of her child going on to develop a full mutation. Normal transmitting males can also be detected.

It is critically important for genetic counselors and other health care professionals to be conscious of how devastating a diagnosis of fragile X syndrome or other inherited diseases can be. Many families report not being able to pay attention during the initial sessions because of the upsetting and painful nature of the information. Many parents are depressed and angry for weeks afterwards. It may be useful to prepare the family slowly by letting them know that you have some upsetting news and wondering with them how to best go about telling them. In some cases, brief psychotherapy may be useful. Other families may wish to bring along a trusted relative, minister, rabbi, or close friend to hear the news and to question the doctors on the family's behalf. In every case, care should be taken concerning the words initially used to describe the syndrome. Certain words, such as *mutation,* can add unnecessarily to the families' trauma.

Prevention and Reproductive Choices

Genetic counseling is best done before a pregnancy occurs. If, however, a pregnancy is under way, the couple may elect to have one of two diagnostic procedures. Chorionic villus biopsy is a procedure in which a small amount of the tissue from the developing placenta is collected. Amniocentesis involves collecting some of the fluid that surrounds the fetus. Either one of these samples may be used to detect the genetic status of the fetus—including whether it has a full or pre-mutation—with a high degree of accuracy. Both procedures are associated with complications in a small percentage of cases.

More precise information, however, may not always make childbearing decisions any easier, and may lead to new dilemmas for some families. It may be more clear to some couples than others whether or not they choose to continue a pregnancy of a fetus that is fully affected with the syndrome. Decisions may become less clear in other cases, as when the baby has a pre-mutation and would develop normally, but their children and/or grandchildren would be at a very high risk for having fragile X syndrome.

Once carrier females and, less frequently, normal transmitting males, have been identified, it is not yet clear how they arrive at their reproductive decisions. Some couples choose to have children regardless of the associated risks, or to obtain abortions of affected fetuses. Other couples elect not to bear children, deciding instead to adopt, remain childless, or use alternative reproductive techniques (Black, 1992). These alternative techniques include donor eggs for carrier females and donor sperm for carrier males at risk for transmitting the fragile X marker to their daughters. An additional, newly developed choice involves preimplantation testing, or actually performing molecular testing for fragile X syndrome in one or two cells of an in vitro fertilized embryo, followed by implantation of embryos without the disorder (Levinson et al., 1992). Various forms of gene therapy may be possible in the future.

Although research has not yet established how couples choose among these multiple reproductive alternatives, preliminary work has identified several features that are associated with the decision of carrier females to bear children. Most carrier women want prenatal diagnosis, and carrier females who already have one affected fragile X child are more likely to terminate an affected pregnancy than carrier women without children (Meryash & Abuelo, 1988). Meryash (1992) has also found that carrier women who would consider abortion are more educated and less likely to be Catholic than women who would not consider this option. Women considering abortion were also more concerned about the impact that an affected child might have on the quality of life for existing family members, including other children, themselves, and their relationships with their husbands. Subjects in Meryash's (1992) study who were certain of their decision to abort or not had a greater knowledge of fragile X and relied more heavily on advice from their physicians than women who were unsure of their abortion decision.

Other, as yet unexplored, variables may also affect reproductive decisions. Research has yet to consider, for example, if women's actual behavior when confronted with a pregnancy differs from their hypothetical solutions. In addition, research needs to specify how childbearing decisions are affected by the presence or absence of cognitive impairment and emotional problems in these women. The role of the father in childbearing decisions also remains unknown.

The emotional impact of the fragile X diagnosis on immediate and extended family members is considerable. Some families, especially parents of older fragile X persons, may experience an element of "relief" in finally having an explanation of their child's difficulties. Yet despite this relief, many parents also blame themselves, become angry and/or depressed, anguish over how and when to tell other family members, and vacillate between being hopeful about and fearing the worst for their child's future. Families need support and guidance both during and after the diagnostic process; specific ways of providing this support are described in Chapter 8.

SUMMARY

Since Martin and Bell's description of an X-linked disorder in the early 1940s, advances in the molecular basis of fragile X syndrome have literally revolutionized this field and led to the development of highly accurate and precise diagnostic tests. These tests may be used to screen both at-risk groups and the general population for full and pre-mutations of the fragile X syndrome. Within affected families, however, such precise information may not make reproductive decisions any easier.

To date, fragile X is one of only three genetic disorders in which a nucleotide triplet is amplified to an extraordinary degree, beginning with a "pre-mutation" and progressing across generations to a full mutation. Although the mechanisms responsible for this amplification are unknown, future advances in molecular genetics are likely to illuminate the process more completely. It is now known that a null mutation of the *FMR-1* gene is responsible for the clinical picture seen in fragile X males and females. We now turn to this clinical description and how fragile X is manifest within several domains of behavior.

3

PHYSICAL FEATURES

Fragile X syndrome is similar to other genetic causes of mental retardation (e.g., Down syndrome, Prader-Willi syndrome) in that it results in distinctive physical features. Although physical features in fragile X syndrome vary across affected individuals, they nevertheless occur frequently enough to help professionals identify potential fragile X males in schools, clinics, and other settings. This chapter is divided by gender because physical features in fragile X syndrome differ by sex and are more apparent in males than females.

MALES

Certain physical features have long been considered "classic" of fragile X males. These characteristic include a long, narrow face; long, thick, prominent ears; and possibly a prominent forehead and jaw (see Figure 3.1). Although these features have been noted in up to 80% of fragile X males, they are not always consistently observed. Moreover, early observations suggested that some young fragile X boys do not necessarily show excessively large ears or a long face because these features may become more pronounced with age (Brondum-Nielsen, 1988). Rather, some young boys were noted to have a puffy face with narrow palpebral fissures (or long and narrow eye openings), epicanthal folds (folds at the inner corner of the eyes), and a large head relative to their body size (e.g., Hockey & Crowhurst, 1988; Simko, Hornstein, Soukup, & Bagamery, 1989).

More recent research, however, has compared ear length and head circumference in fragile X males throughout their developmental years with well-established normative data from unaffected males (Butler, Brunschwig, Miller, & Hagerman, 1992). This research shows that ear length in fragile X males is above the normal percentiles at all ages, and

Figure 3.1. Facial Features in 33-Year-Old Identical Twin Males With Fragile X Syndrome

head circumference, also above normal percentiles, is apt to be particularly pronounced in boys 6 months through 6 years of age. Figures 3.2 and 3.3 depict these features in three young fragile X boys. Figures 3.1 and 3.2 are of the same fragile X males, identical twins, whose large ears are apparent as both children and adults.

In addition to these facial characteristics, macroorchidism, or large testes, has also long been considered a classic feature of fragile X syndrome. Macroorchidism is encountered in 80% to 96% of postpubertal males, and in a much smaller number of prepubertal boys, approximately 20% to 24% (Lachiewicz, 1992b; Sutherland & Hecht, 1985; Turner, Daniel, & Frost, 1980). Butler et al. (1992), however, observed that testicular volume in fragile X males was above the normal percentiles at all ages, and that after age 6, boys showed dramatic increases in testicular volume. Although macroorchidism is also found in many other

Figure 3.2. Facial Features of the Men in Figure 3.1 as 6-Year-Old Boys

mentally retarded adults, excessively large testicular volumes have differentiated fragile X from other institutionalized males (Kirkilionis, Pozsonyi, & Sergovich, 1988).

Other unusual growth patterns have been inconsistently reported in fragile X syndrome, including above average birth weight, proneness to obesity, and among adults, either short stature or increased height (Brondum-Nielsen, 1988; Loesch, Lafranchi, & Scott, 1988; Partington, 1984; Sutherland & Hecht, 1985). Butler et al.'s (1992) recent work clarifies some of these inconsistencies. Specifically, it appears that the height of fragile X males follows normal growth curves until age 15, at which point they begin to fall below normal percentiles. Similarly, weight seems to follow normal percentiles until age 12; after this age fragile X males show a proneness to obesity that remits around age 20, when they fall below normal percentiles for weight.

Variability in growth patterns and the high frequency of macroorchidism have led to speculation about thyroid and endocrine dysfunction in

Figure 3.3. Facial Features in an 8-Year-Old Boy With Fragile X Syndrome

fragile X syndrome. Subtle abnormalities in the hypothalamic-pituitary axis have been found in some fragile X males (Bregman, Leckman, & Ort, 1990), yet such anomalies may not be unique to fragile X syndrome (Wilson, Carpenter, & Berkovitz, 1988).

TABLE 3.1 Physical Features of Males With Fragile X Syndrome

Physical Feature	Percentages	References
Macro-orchidism	80 – 96	1, 5, 9, 16, 17
Large or prominent ears	50 – 75	1, 3, 5, 11
Long face	60 – 83	1, 3, 6, 11
Hyperextensible joints	57 – 79	1, 2, 3, 5
High arched palate	40 – 65	1, 2, 3, 5
Abnormal hand dermatoglyphics	35 – 51	3, 10, 12, 13
Abnormal foot dermatoglyphics	75 – 90	6, 10
Flat feet	50 – 65	2, 3
Mitral valve prolapse	22 – 55	7, 14
Pectus excavatum	32 – 45	3, 5, 6
Strabismus	30 – 56	8, 15
Otitis media	45 – 63	4, 11

Note: References for Table: 1. Bregman, Dykens, Watson, Ort, & Leckman, 1987; 2. Davids, Hagerman, & Eilert, 1990; 3. Hagerman, 1991; 4. Hagerman, Altshul-Stark, & McBogg, 1987; 5. Hagerman, Smith, & Mariner, 1983; 6. Lachiewicz, 1992b; 7. Loehr, Synhorst, Wolfe, & Hagerman, 1986; 8. Maino, Wesson, Schlange, Cibis, & Maino, 1991; 9. Partington, 1984; 10. Rodewald et al., 1986; 11. Simko, Hornstein, Soukup, & Bagamery, 1989; 12. Simpson, 1986; 13. Simpson, Newman, & Partington, 1984; 14. Sreeman, Wren, Bhate, Robertson, & Hunter, 1989; 15. Storm, PeBenito, & Ferretti, 1987; 16. Sutherland & Hecht, 1985; 17. Turner, Brookwell, Daniel, Selikowitz, & Zilibowitz, 1980. Percentages are the lowest and highest figures reported among studies.

Other features are also often but not always found in fragile X males. As indicated in Table 3.1, these features include a high arched palate that may also be associated with dental crowding in some older males; hyperextensible joints, especially in prepubescent boys; soft, velvet, hyperelastic skin; hypotonia (floppy muscle tone), especially in younger boys, which occasionally may be associated with sucking problems in infancy; mitral valve (heart) prolapse; flat feet; pectus excavatum (a sunken chest); abnormal dermatoglyphics of the hands (e.g., Sydney and Simian creases, whorls, and loops) and of the feet (e.g., hallucal creases). These characteristics, along with macroorchidism and large ears, have supported earlier observations of an underlying connective tissue disorder in fragile X syndrome (e.g., Opitz, Westphal, & Daniel, 1984).

In addition to manifestations of a connective tissue disorder, some fragile X males show vision and hearing problems. The primary visual problem seems to be strabismus, or combining and directing gaze with both eyes (Maino, Wesson, Schlange, Cibis, & Maino, 1991; Storm, PeBenito, & Ferretti, 1987). Recurrent otitis media, or chronic ear infections, are a common source of hearing difficulties, especially in younger boys (Hagerman, Altshul-Stark, & McBogg, 1987; Simko et al., 1989).

It remains unclear whether these visual and auditory problems in fragile X boys affect their subsequent development in cognition, speech, or language.

Magnetic resonance imaging (MRI) of the brains of a small number of fragile X subjects has thus far revealed slightly smaller midline cerebellar structures and enlarged fourth ventricles (a cavity filled with cerebrospinal fluid above the brain stem), yet these findings may not be specific to fragile X syndrome (Reiss, 1988). Postmortem brain studies suggest abnormal-appearing dendritic spines of the pyramidal neurons in the neocortex. Although such abnormalities may be consistent with neurobehavioral deficits, both the MRI and post mortem studies are preliminary given the small number of subjects studied.

FEMALES

There are considerably fewer obvious physical features in fragile X females than males; in addition, these features have been described as more subtle. Similar to males, fragile X females may show many of the "classic" physical features noted above. Fryns (1986), for example, found that 28% of 125 carrier females had a long face, and prominent forehead and jaw. These features, as well as large ears were also observed by Cronister et al. (1991) and Loesch and Hay (1988).

As in males, the developmental aspects of these features have been described. Many young girls with fragile X syndrome show the large ears and long faces characteristic of their male counterparts (Borghgraef, Fryns, & Van den Berghe, 1990; Hagerman, Jackson et al., 1992). Although Borghgraef et al. (1990) suggest an overgrowth syndrome in their sample of seven girls, Hagerman, Jackson et al. (1992) found no differences in the head circumference, height, or weight in 32 fragile X positive girls compared to their unaffected, fragile X negative sisters.

Also as in males, the presence of both connective tissue problems and thyroid-endocrine abnormalities has been implicated in females. Cronister et al. (1991) found that hyperextensible joints distinguished impaired fragile X women from a non-fragile X control group, thus lending some support for connective tissue problems in females as well as males.

Preliminary data also suggest some anomalies in the reproductive and ovarian functioning of fragile X women that may parallel subtle abnormalities in thyroid and endocrine functioning found in males. Fryns (1986) found high fertility rates among carrier females, especially among cognitively impaired women, including a fourfold increase in the number of women who gave birth to twins relative to the rate of twinning in the general population. In spite of these findings, an increased frequency of miscarriages has been noted among carrier females (Loesch & Hay, 1988). Cronister et al. (1991) found premature menopause in 13% of their sample of normal IQ carrier women compared to only 5% in their non-fragile X control subjects. These researchers also identified other ovarian problems in both affected and unaffected fragile X females (e.g., ovarian cysts and tumors) that are in need of further study.

In contrast to males, virtually every study with females has shown that unusual physical features are more prevalent among intellectually impaired than average IQ women. Fryns (1986) found that a long face and a prominent forehead and jaw were more common among carrier females with borderline intelligence, or mild-moderate mental retardation. Similarly, Loesch and Hay (1988) noted that facial features, as well as hyperextensible joints and flat feet, were more prominent among cognitively impaired women. Cronister et al. (1991) noted that some physical features were present in 20% of their average IQ carrier females, yet they too confirmed the association between the number of unusual physical features and intellectual level.

SUMMARY

Because physical features are generally more variable and subtle among fragile X females, there is more agreement as to a "classic" physical phenotype among fragile X males. Many of these physical features, including height, weight, ear length, head circumference, and testicular volume, change throughout development, and as such, are consistent with certain behavioral characteristics that also become more or less pronounced at different ages. The biological basis for the emergence of these features remains to be established.

Although many of the "classic" physical features of fragile X syndrome are quite striking (e.g., prominent ears and macroorchidism), the complete description of persons with fragile X syndrome extends beyond their physical characteristics and includes an appreciation of their complex behaviors. With this aim in mind, we now turn to the diverse and sometimes controversial findings on behavior in fragile X syndrome.

4

COGNITIVE FUNCTIONING

Deficits in cognitive functioning, along with adaptive behavior (see Chapter 6), are key components in the definition of mental retardation. As established by intelligence testing, an intelligence quotient (IQ) of less than 70 is the usual cut-off point that is necessary for a diagnosis of mental retardation (Grossman, 1983).

IQ levels for affected males with fragile X syndrome range from mild to moderate mental retardation to profound and severe levels of impairment (IQs less than 50). It is estimated, however, that approximately 20% of males who carry the pre-mutation of the fragile X gene do not have mental retardation (Sherman et al., 1984). In addition, approximately one third of heterozygous fragile X females show some degree of learning difficulties (e.g., Turner, Brookwell, Daniel, Selikowitz, & Zilibowitz, 1980).

In contrast to other genetic disorders, however, research in fragile X syndrome has gone beyond the simple documentation of intellectual deficit. Research has now identified characteristic cognitive strengths and weaknesses in fragile X males, and how intelligence changes over time. Females with fragile X syndrome also have received a great deal of attention recently, and preliminary ties are now being made between the intellectual functioning of these women and the new genetic classifications based on the extent of the mutation (pre-mutation versus full mutation).

PROFILES, SPECIFICITY, AND TRAJECTORIES

Three issues characterize most work on intelligence in fragile X syndrome. The first involves intellectual profiles, or those aspects of intelligence that are particularly weak or strong. The second concerns whether such strengths and weaknesses differ from intellectual profiles found in other groups of mentally retarded persons. The third relates to the trajectory of IQ over time, whether development is steady or variable as the child gets older. This chapter first discusses these issues in affected males with the full mutation, and then in carrier females.

Intelligence in Males With Fragile X Syndrome

Profiles of Cognitive Functioning. Earliest studies of cognitive functioning in affected males with fragile X syndrome hinted at certain characteristic intellectual strengths and weaknesses. Using the Wechsler Adult Intelligence Scale-Revised (WAIS-R; Wechsler, 1981), Chudley (1984) found that males with fragile X syndrome showed some strengths in visual memory, attention to visual detail, and verbal concept formation, and weaknesses in auditory memory. Herbst, Dunn, Dill, Kalousek, and Krywaniuk (1981) also reported that males with fragile X have particular difficulty with short-term memory for digits, as well as numerical reasoning.

Although these early studies pointed to specific, relative strengths and weaknesses, they did not provide an overarching construct with which to better understand the cognitive deficits seen in fragile X syndrome. More recently, better characterizations of the cognitive deficits of males with this disorder have come about through research on their *styles* of information processing as opposed to discrete cognitive abilities.

To provide a brief background, there has traditionally been a dichotomy in the field of intelligence between theories of general intelligence and theories that emphasize specific factors or domains of abilities. In contrast to the search for general or separate abilities, Das, Kirby, and Jarman (1975) have examined particular "styles" of solving problems. Consistent with Soviet neurologist Luria, Das and his colleagues (1975) proposed that there are two styles of information processing: *simultaneous processing,* which involves integrating stimuli in a holistic, frequently spatial, gestalt-like manner (e.g., recognizing a picture even though a line is missing), and *sequential processing,* or placing information in step-by-step serial or temporal order (e.g., words in a sentence, short-term memory tasks).

The distinction between sequential and simultaneous processing has an advantage over other approaches in that there may be particular brain correlates of each type of functioning. Das et al. (1975) nominate occipital-parietal lobes as the areas of the brain primarily responsible for simultaneous processing, and the frontal-temporal regions as responsible for sequential processing.

Due to the appeal of the mental processing approach, Kaufman and Kaufman (1983) designed an intelligence test, the Kaufman Assessment Battery for Children, or K-ABC, to tap sequential and simultaneous processing in 2½- to 12½-year-old children. In addition to assessing these two processing domains, the K-ABC also contains a separate measure of academic achievement and acquired information (e.g., vocabulary, reading, arithmetic). The organization of the K-ABC into the two processing scales versus the achievement scale differs from other IQ tests. This division is based on yet another theory of intelligence that involves fluid abilities (relatively culture-free mental operations) versus crystallized abilities (knowledge and acquired skills that are culturally dependent).

In the first study to use the K-ABC with fragile X males, Dykens, Hodapp, and Leckman (1987) discovered that fragile X subjects performed particularly poorly on Sequential Processing tasks. The markedly depressed level of Sequential Processing was demonstrated by all subjects, with differences between Sequential and Simultaneous Processing ranging from 1 to 3.83 years (mean = 2.17 years) across individual subjects.

In addition to the weakness in Sequential Processing, Dykens et al. (1987) noted a particular pattern of strengths and weaknesses within each of the three domains. Although the entire Sequential Processing domain was weak for these subjects, their performances were even more impaired on Sequential Processing's Hand Movements subtest, a visual-motor, short-term memory task in which the subject must replicate a series of hand movements. Conversely, within the domain of Simultaneous Processing, these males showed relative strengths in a task assessing perceptual closure and long-term memory (Gestalt Closure), and weaknesses in a subtest tapping visual-spatial short-term memory (Spatial Memory). Among the Achievement subtests, Arithmetic was a relative weakness.

These findings from the Dykens et al. (1987) study were replicated in a second study using the K-ABC with 4- to 12-year-old fragile X boys (Kemper, Hagerman, & Altshul-Stark, 1988). Despite some slight differences between the two K-ABC studies, results from these separate research groups were remarkably similar. Collectively, they indicate that fragile X males have particular difficulties in sequential processing, which are likely to be associated with their weaknesses in arithmetic. These weaknesses, as well as relative strengths in certain aspects of simultaneous processing, have significant implications for the development of appropriate teaching strategies and interventions with fragile X males. These strategies are described in detail in Chapter 8.

Etiologic Specificity. Weaknesses in sequential processing and strengths in simultaneous processing may be specific to fragile X syndrome, or they may be shown by other groups of mentally retarded persons. From research conducted to date, it does appear that the fragile X cognitive profile is relatively specific. Studies of mildly impaired children with cultural-familial retardation or with learning disabilities show no particular pattern of intellectual strengths and weaknesses on the K-ABC (Naglieri, 1985; Obrzut, Nelson, & Obrzut, 1987). Similarly, Pueschel, Gallagher, Zartler, and Pezzullo (1987) found that subjects with Down syndrome showed almost identical levels of Sequential and Simultaneous Processing on the K-ABC. Despite this even profile, Pueschel et al. (1987) found that children with Down syndrome showed a marked strength in the Hand Movements subtest relative to other K-ABC tasks. In contrast, Hand Movements was the single most depressed subtest for boys with fragile X syndrome.

In a more rigorous test of the specificity issue, Hodapp, Leckman et al. (1992) directly compared K-ABC profiles in fragile X males to Down syndrome and "nonspecific" mentally retarded boys matched on both chronological and mental ages. As expected, males with fragile X syndrome demonstrated a pronounced deficit in Sequential Processing relative to both Simultaneous Processing and Achievement. Also, consistent with Pueschel et al. (1987), Down syndrome boys demonstrated almost identical functioning in Sequential and Simultaneous Processing. In contrast to earlier studies of children with mixed etiologies, however, the nonspecific group showed a weakness in Sequential Processing. Unlike their fragile X counterparts, the nonspecific group did not manifest any relative strengths. Although the reasons for these findings among the nonspecific group remain unclear, it may be that some of these boys, who did not receive genetic testing, actually had fragile X syndrome.

In research to date, then, there does appear to be some degree of specificity to the fragile X cognitive profile. Males with fragile X syndrome differ in their profiles from Down syndrome boys, and from the evenly developed processing scores shown in most studies of nonspecific groups, although some of these subjects may show a partial "fragile X like" profile. Although more work is needed with other etiological and nonspecific groups, the disorder's marked weaknesses in sequential processing and strengths in simultaneous processing appear to be "etiology-specific" for fragile X syndrome.

This cognitive profile in fragile X syndrome suggests the presence of neuropsychological mechanisms that are specific to the fragile X group.

Although several neuropsychological mechanisms have been advanced, the best hypothesis to date is the possibility that fragile X individuals have deficits in prefrontal lobe functioning. Recall that Das et al. (1975) nominated frontal-temporal areas of the brain as responsible for performance on sequential processing tasks. This possibility has been further specified in Goldman-Rakic's (1987) work on adult primates.

In a series of primate experiments, Goldman-Rakic (1987) has localized the prefrontal cortex as the area of the brain responsible for short-term memory, planning, and attention—all thought to be especially delayed in persons with fragile X syndrome. Specifically, monkeys with lesions in their frontal cortex fail tasks in which they must keep in mind the desired response over delays of several seconds. These types of tasks—in both primates and humans—tap functioning in executive abilities that require maintaining a response set. Set maintenance is important in impulse control, strategic planning, making goals, self-monitoring, anticipation, and flexibility in thought and action.

Although not yet fully explored, Goldman-Rakic's (1987) findings regarding the frontal cortex may provide an analogue for the deficits in attention, short-term memory, and planning often seen in fragile X syndrome (Pennington, O'Connor, & Sudhalter, 1991). It remains unknown whether a deficit in prefrontal functioning is the only or primary deficit in fragile X syndrome, or whether prefrontal deficits alone can account for the majority of etiology-specific behaviors. Despite these unknown issues, deficits in prefrontal functioning provide a useful model for pulling together certain features of fragile X males, including problems with attention and sequential processing.

Developmental Course of Cognitive Functioning. The trajectory of intellectual functioning in fragile X syndrome has received much attention. In particular, researchers have determined whether males with fragile X syndrome develop at a steady rate or whether their rates of intellectual development might change at different points in time.

Rate of intellectual development appears to differ based on the individual's etiology of mental retardation. When children with unknown or mixed etiologies are examined, developmental rates appear relatively constant. Testing children with educable mental retardation at yearly intervals, Silverstein (1982) found that average Stanford-Binet IQs were virtually identical (IQs 64-67) from ages 11 through 14. Similarly, in a follow-up study of the adult functioning of children in special education classes, Ross, Begab, Dondis, Giampiccolo, and Meyers (1985) found that their data "argue strongly for IQ stability" (p. 69) over an inter-test interval of 35 years. In studies of specific etiological groups, results are more variable. Persons with Prader-Willi syndrome show apparent stability in IQ scores throughout their childhood and adult years (Dykens, Hodapp, Walsh, & Nash, 1992b). In contrast, in Down syndrome, rates of intellectual development become increasingly slower as children get older (Hodapp & Zigler, 1990). Much of this decline in Down syndrome appears to occur in the earliest years, although IQ declines also may occur later in development.

Fragile X males present a startling contrast to groups with nonspecific etiologies, Prader-Willi syndrome, or Down syndrome. Early cross-sectional reports (assessing different subjects across various age groups) suggested that IQ levels might decline with age. In particular, males with fragile X syndrome were often noted to be in the mild and borderline levels of retardation as children, but in the moderately and severely retarded ranges as adults. Until recently, however, it remained possible that selection or test biases might be producing an artifact of declining intellectual rates in fragile X syndrome.

To address this possibility, there now have been five studies that have longitudinally examined intellectual development in fragile X males. These five longitudinal studies assessed their respective subjects at different points in time, providing a more rigorous measure of development than cross-sectional approaches. Despite this similarity, these studies differed in a number of ways: some used the same IQ tests and some different IQ tests for the first and second testing (using z-score transformations to equate different tests), and each differed in the number of fragile X males tested, the ages at which these children were examined, and the interval from first to second testing.

Table 4.1 shows the findings of these five major studies. There is a remarkable consistency of findings: On average, the IQs of males with fragile X syndrome decline as these boys get older. This decline in the rate of intellectual advance can be seen despite the many differences across the various studies.

A second, more tentative, conclusion is that the decline in IQ shown by many fragile X males is not linear over time. Unlike Down syndrome, few studies in fragile X syndrome have found declines during the early years. Although Lachiewicz, Gullion, Spiridigliozzi, and Aylsworth (1987) consider the declines to occur relatively evenly over time, they found few declines among their subjects tested two times before age 10. Hagerman

TABLE 4.1 Major Studies of IQ Change in Fragile X Syndrome

Study	N	Age at Testing 1st	Age at Testing 2nd	Age at Testing 3rd	IQ at Testing 1st	IQ at Testing 2nd	IQ at Testing 3rd	Other Information	Findings and Comments
Lachiewicz et al. (1987)	21	5.59 (2.8-8.5)	12.48 (5.0-19.7)	—	59.5	45.9	—	Longitudinal study; different IQ tests used in 1st & 2nd testing for 10 of 21 Ss; equating of diff IQ tests through z-scores.	IQ declines from test 1 to 2; 13 of 21 Ss showed sig IQ declines. 11 of 15 retested after 10 years showed sig declines. Only 2 of 6 retested before 10 showed these declines.
Dykens, Hodapp, Ort et al. (1989)	56							X-sectional study shows IQ declines from 5-10 to 10-15, & from 15-20; stable to 20-25 & 25-30.	IQ declines from tests 1 to 2 to 3. Mixture X-sectional & longitudinal studies show diff pts of decline over time. Declines from 5-10 to 10-15 to 15-20, not before or after.
	10	5-10	10-15	15-20	53.8	47.2	40.6	Longitudinal study; mean IQ from multiple testings during each age period. 8 of 10 Ss received S-Bs at each testing, 1 WISC, 1 mixed.	
Hagerman et al. (1989)	24	11.42 (4.5-29.0)	16.27 (7.6-33.2)	—	54.9	48.4	—	Longitudinal study using S-Bs for all Ss.	IQ declines from test 1 to 2; only 7 of 24 Ss showed sig decline over time. Ss with longer intertest intervals more likely to show sig declines. Age 6 or 7 thought to begin IQ decline.

(Continued)

TABLE 4.1 (Continued)

Study	N	Age at Testing			IQ at Testing			Other Information	Findings and Comments
		1st	2nd	3rd	1st	2nd	3rd		
Hodapp, Dykens et al. (1990)	66	9.21 (3-18)	12.68 (5-20)	—	53.3	47.3	—	Longitudinal, multicenter study; Ss from first 3 studies where S was tested 2x w/same test.	IQ declines from test 1 to 2; bigger decreases in Ss posttested during 10-15 or 15-20 year periods. Some IQ declines in high-IQ Ss before age 10, but may be due to regression effects.
Fisch et al. (1991)	60	21.1 (2.6-53.7)	27.0 (4.8-56.7)	—	40.1	35.8	—	Longitudinal, multicenter study w/older & institution-alized Ss from U.S., Germany, Japan, & Belgium. 28 of 60 Ss pretested age 20; only 19 lived at home.	IQ declines from tests 1 to 2; bigger decreases when longer intervals between testing.

et al. (1989) hypothesize that IQ declines begin from about age 8 onward, whereas Dykens, Hodapp et al. (1989) and Hodapp, Dykens et al. (1990) identify the age period from about 10 to 15 as the beginning of the decline in rate of intellectual development.

Given that there may be different ages at which IQs decline in males with fragile X syndrome, why might these declines occur? To date, several reasons have been proposed. Hagerman et al. (1989) hypothesize that the IQ decline in the later portion of middle childhood is due to inherent properties of IQ tests and to increasing numbers of more difficult items on these tests. These researchers note that, "as higher cognitive functions are depended upon in the middle childhood years, fragile X children have a more difficult time in testing. More complex directions are given, and more complex definitions are required for success" (p. 517).

In contrast, Dykens, Hodapp et al. (1989) consider the declines as beginning at slightly later ages (10-15 years as opposed to 8-10 years) and hypothesize that "the regulatory factors responsible for the initiation of puberty may play an important role in the plateauing of mental age (MA) seen in these subjects" (p. 425). For example, in the normal course of development, the fragile X gene may be "turned on" in a special way with the beginning of puberty so that boys with a null mutation of the gene again will be adversely affected. This effect might involve similar mechanisms that underlie the marked hypertrophy of the testes that begins in earnest in early puberty.

The two hypotheses offered by Hagerman et al. (1989) and Dykens, Hodapp et al. (1989) represent two possibilities for changes in intellectual rates seen in the larger mental retardation field (Hodapp & Burack, 1990). These changes involve the difference between "task-related" versus "age-related" slowings of development.

Task-related slowing occurs when children of a particular etiology of mental retardation slow in development because of syndrome-specific difficulties in mastering particular developmental tasks. In young children with Down syndrome, for example, Dunst (1990) found that these children decreased in their rate of development as they progressed from one Piagetian sensorimotor stage to another. These decreases in rate of development were found across stages even when the already slowed developmental rate of Down syndrome children had been taken into account. These children thus were slowed down by many (not all) of the different "tasks" of sensorimotor functioning.

In contrast, *chronological-age slowing* involves a slowing in rate of development that is based on the particular chronological age of the child.

In Down syndrome, for example, several researchers have discovered a temporary plateau in grammatical, adaptive, and intellectual development in subjects between the ages of about 7 and 11 (Dykens, Hodapp, & Evans, 1992; Fowler, 1988; Gibson 1966). Although the mechanisms remain unclear, most Down syndrome children show such chronological age-related slowing during these middle-childhood years.

Although the issue remains open, the present authors favor the second, or age-related, model as the predominant factor in the slowing of development seen in fragile X syndrome. Most fragile X boys—of whatever level of impairment—appear to slow in development during the pubertal years, thereby calling into question a task-related explanation. It thus may be beneficial to emphasize the acquisition of cognitive skills prior to the onset of age-related neurobiological changes; a recommendation that is discussed further in Chapter 8. In addition, unlike Down syndrome, in which slowing occurs in response to problems in mastering certain sensorimotor tasks, the specific tasks hypothesized to slow fragile X males remain unclear. Yet the chronological-age slowing hypothesis also requires greater specification, especially the neurobiological factors that are associated with such slowing.

Further support for age-related as opposed to task-related slowing of development is found in preliminary observations by Reiss (1992) of changes in the brain structure of fragile X males. Specifically, Reiss (1992) has noted that there may be age-related declines in the proportion of "gray matter" (or nerve cell bodies) to brain size that becomes more pronounced in males above age 10. In addition, both males and females may show age-related decreases in the actual size of parts of the temporal lobe (involved in auditory perception and language comprehension). Although tantalizing, this work does not indicate *why* these changes in the brain occur, only that they appear to occur concurrently with slowing rates of cognitive development at or around the 10-year period. Although age-related shifts in the proportions and structures of the brain are not yet sufficiently elaborated, these preliminary observations provide a promising explanation of the age-related decline in IQ observed in many fragile X males.

Combining Profiles and Rates. So far, the issues of profiles and rates of intelligence in males with fragile X syndrome have been examined separately. Recent evidence, however, suggests that the sequential processing deficit often seen in fragile X males becomes more pronounced with increasing chronological age, thereby linking together the issues of cognitive profiles and rates of development.

Age-related changes in the intensity of various physical and behavioral features are often seen in mental retardation. Babies with Prader-Willi syndrome, for example, show hypotonia, as well as sucking problems, and lack of interest in food, followed by marked preoccupation with food and hyperphagia (overeating) in early childhood. Behaviorally, children with Down syndrome often show relative strengths in pragmatics and vocabulary that intensify at various chronological ages (Fowler, 1988).

In fragile X syndrome as well, there appears to be an intensification of the disorder's etiology-specific strengths and weaknesses. In a study using the K-ABC with 5- to 28-year-old fragile X males, Hodapp, Dykens, Ort, Zelinsky, and Leckman (1991) found relationships between increasing age and higher scores on several Achievement and Simultaneous Processing subtests; no such relationships were found with Sequential Processing tasks. Longitudinally, both younger and older males tested twice with the K-ABC showed gains in Simultaneous Processing and in Achievement, although gains were less striking in the post-10-year period. In contrast, test-retest data in Sequential Processing showed modest increases during the pre-10-year period, with no increases whatsoever in those subjects tested twice in the post-10-year period. Although rates of cognitive development thus slowed in all three domains after age 10, the development of sequential skills stopped totally. As a result, Sequential Processing— already the weakest domain for males with fragile X syndrome—became an area of even greater deficit during the postpubertal years.

INTELLIGENCE IN FEMALES WITH FRAGILE X SYNDROME

There has been a recent flurry of research on the intellectual functioning of women who carry the full mutation or the silent pre-mutation. This research has made considerable progress in joining new genetic findings to the intellectual profiles of these girls and women; a pattern that is likely to continue in the years ahead.

It has long been known that females with cytogenetically confirmed fragile X syndrome can either be affected or unaffected carriers. The affected carriers typically have the full mutation, while the unaffected carriers have the silent pre-mutation. The range of clinical presentation of the girls and women with the full mutation varies considerably, with most of these females showing learning disabilities, and others showing either mild mental retardation (with IQs from 55 to 70) or cognitive functioning that falls in the Borderline range of intelligence (with IQs from 71 to 84) (Fryns, 1986).

In considering the full range of expression in affected females (those with IQs of 84 and below), the critical issue seems to be whether the fragile X gene is transcribed, and the *FMR-1* protein is made or not. Those women with a full mutation are likely to be affected to one degree or another along a spectrum of cognitive problems that range from learning disabilities to mild mental retardation. As described in Chapter 2, once the full mutation is present, the factors that are likely to affect the final result are the proportion of brain cells in particular brain locations that fail to express the fragile X protein or not. Thus those women in which the affected X chromosome is the functional X chromosome in most of their brain cells will more closely resemble the affected males, whereas those carrier females with the full mutation but in which relatively fewer brain cells are relying on the affected X chromosome will have only mild cognitive difficulties.

Consistent with these hypotheses, affected fragile X females do seem to show profiles of cognitive strengths and weaknesses that resemble to one degree or another the profiles shown by their male counterparts.

In much the same way as with affected males, the early studies of affected fragile X females identified aspects of intellectual functioning that were particularly weak or strong. For example, many reports noted that verbal IQs were often elevated over performance IQs in females with fragile X syndrome (e.g., Cianchetti et al., 1991; Loesch & Hay, 1988) whereas other studies have not found this pattern (e.g., Brainerd, Schreiner, & Hagerman, 1991).

Many of these females are similar to males in that their skills in arithmetic and in auditory memory fall below their overall levels of intellectual abilities (Miezjeski et al., 1986). This deficit in auditory memory—usually measured by tasks requiring immediate recall of digits—may suggest similar short-term memory and attentional problems as those seen in males with fragile X syndrome.

Unlike their male counterparts, many affected females seem to have deficits in visual-spatial functioning and perceptual planning abilities. These weaknesses have been manifest in the WAIS-R Block Design subtest, in copying designs from the Benton Visual-Motor test, and in nonverbal intelligence tests such as Raven's Progressive Matrices (e.g., Cianchetti et al., 1991; Grigsby, Kemper, Hagerman, & Myers, 1990; Loesch & Hay, 1988).

Recent work also has established that many affected females show problems in tasks involving so-called executive functions that are typically associated with the frontal lobe of the brain (e.g., Freund & Baumgardner, 1992). These executive functions include features such as planning, attending, sustaining effort, generating problem-solving strategies, using feedback, self-monitoring, and shifting responses. In a study comparing affected carriers with unaffected carriers and with mothers of children who have other disabilities, Mazzocco, Hagerman, Cronister-Silverman, and Pennington (1992) found that affected carriers performed worse on measures of these executive functions than remaining groups. Yet on measures of verbal, nonverbal, and long-term memory functioning, these affected carriers performed equally to the other two groups.

Several weaknesses thus characterize cognitive profiles in affected females with fragile X syndrome, including many features that are associated with the frontal lobe: math, attention, short-term memory, visual-spatial functioning, planning, generating problem-solving strategies, and using feedback. Other areas, such as vocabulary, long-term memory, and verbal abilities, appear much less impaired.

Although there is little work on the trajectory of intelligence in fragile X females, Hagerman, Jackson et al. (1992) longitudinally examined the IQs of 12 cytogenetically positive girls. These researchers found that girls demonstrated steady intellectual development, at least until the mid-teen years, perhaps because some brain cells continue to make the *FMR-1* protein. Thus, in contrast to the declines in IQ found in males with fragile X, females with this disorder seem to be developing at a slow but steady pace during the childhood years. Further studies with larger groups of females across a wider age range are needed to confirm these preliminary findings.

Unaffected Carrier Females

As implied in the review above, many obligate carrier females do not seem to show the consistent difficulties with arithmetic, visual-spatial and perceptual functioning, auditory short-term memory, and "executive" functions demonstrated by affected fragile X females (de von Flint, Bybel, Chudley, & Lopes, 1991). Recent research has suggested that this is due to their having a pre-mutation of the *FMR-1* gene that is transcribed into a full mutation in the egg cells of the mother. Consistent with this view, Hinton et al. (1992) found in a study of unaffected carriers (all of whom had IQs greater than 70) that when carrier females receive the fragile X gene from their fathers, they are a single, homogeneous group: All women show numbers of CGG repeats in the pre-mutation (50-200) range and all have IQs above 85. These women with a pre-mutation of the *FMR-1* gene all performed well on the "Freedom From Distractibility" factor of the WAIS-R, implying that they might not have attentional problems.

In contrast, those women receiving the fragile X gene from their mothers formed two separate subgroups. One such subgroup had IQ scores below 85, had the most CGG repeats, and were cytogenetically positive for fragile X syndrome. The other subgroup had higher IQs (from 85 to 119), showed fewer CGG repeats, and were not cytogenetically positive for fragile X syndrome. For the maternal inheritance group as a whole—particularly for those with lower IQs—deficits were shown in visual-spatial memory and abstraction, and in tasks that required sustained attention. Relative weaknesses in visual memory and attention were also recently reported by Steyaert, Borghgraef, Gaulthier, Fryns, and Van den Berghe (1992) in a group of carrier females with maternal inheritance and average intelligence.

Thus paternal inheritance of the fragile X gene seems to result in daughters who have pre-mutations and an unaffected carrier status. Presumably, the studies cited above that described profiles of strength and weakness among affected carrier females only included fragile X women of maternal inheritance. Females with maternal inheritance may be fully affected carriers (with IQs from 55 to 70) showing prominent patterns of specific cognitive deficits; they may be relatively unaffected cognitively, with IQs from 70 to 84, and showing some indications of specific cognitive difficulties; or they may be completely unaffected cognitively, with IQs of 85 and above, and showing little to no specific cognitive difficulties. As described above, this variation among fragile X females is likely to be associated with the degree to which the X chromosome is activated within brain cells.

Studies to date with carrier females have advanced the field considerably by linking the specific genetic status of these women to differing levels and profiles of cognitive functioning. Replication of some of these studies is needed with larger numbers of subjects who vary across a wider age range. Nonetheless, these studies offer compelling evidence that future research on the cognitive features of carrier females needs to consider the parental source of the fragile X marker, as well as the number of CGG repeats shown by these subjects.

SUMMARY

As a salient component in the definition of mental retardation, deficits in cognitive functioning in fragile X syndrome have been well described. For males with fragile X syndrome, deficits in sequential processing, strengths in certain areas of simultaneous processing, and the declines in IQ at or near puberty may be etiology-specific. Although preliminary, findings that link sequential processing deficits to prefrontal lobe functioning and age-related declines in IQ to shifts in brain proportions and structures are breakthroughs not found in most other syndromes of mental retardation.

Similar to males, affected carrier females may show problems with "executive," prefrontal functions involving planning, attention, short-term memory, math, generating problem-solving strategies, and using feedback. Unlike males, affected carriers may also manifest certain visual-spatial problems. Affected females presumably receive the fragile X gene from their mothers, and although not all females of maternal inheritance show cognitive involvement, those that do vary on a spectrum that ranges from learning disabilities to mild mental retardation. In contrast, carrier females who inherit the fragile X gene from their fathers are cognitively unaffected.

Despite considerable research with both males and females, many features of cognition in fragile X syndrome remain unclear. Studies are needed that specify relationships between cognitive profiles and trajectories, brain structure, and molecular genetic status (i.e., the number of CGG repeats) in both males and females. Further descriptions of the extent to which fragile X profiles and trajectories in both sexes are unique or shared with other groups could also refine the educational and behavioral interventions offered in Chapter 8.

5

SPEECH AND LANGUAGE FUNCTIONING

Early observations of fragile X males noted that their speech was jocular, staccato, perseverative, and sing-songy. Indeed, because this X-linked form of mental retardation seemed associated with particular difficulties in speech, Lehrke (1974) hypothesized that several genes on the X chromosome play an important role in linguistic functioning. More recent research suggests that both the speech and language functioning of fragile X males are deficient even when overall levels of mental retardation are taken into account.

Although linguistic functioning has not received as much research attention as other aspects of behavior, many issues have now been at least partially addressed, including whether fragile X language is an area of deficit relative to overall intellectual abilities, how language abilities relate to functioning in other areas, and how speech and language in fragile X syndrome differs from other types of mental retardation.

Before describing the speech and language functioning of fragile X syndrome, a few features of language in general need to be briefly described. Linguistic skills can be broadly divided into expressive and receptive functioning, or the ability to speak as opposed to understand language. There is some evidence that receptive language may be a strength in many fragile X males relative to their expressive vocabulary skills or overall mental age (e.g., Marans, Paul, & Leckman, 1987; Paul et al., 1987). Expressive vocabulary skills also may be well developed, especially when assessed in situations that offer contextual cues and supports (Sudhalter, Maranion, & Brooks, 1992); a finding consistent with the integrative, contextual learning styles shown by many fragile X males (see Chapters 4 and 8).

In addition to expressive and receptive abilities, other language features that have been researched in fragile X syndrome include:

speech production, including articulation, rate of speech, and prosody (or the melody of speech);

syntax, or the grammatical ordering of words in sentences, and producing or understanding complicated sentences such as declaratives, questions, and conditionals; and

pragmatics, or the use of language for its many communicative functions. Pragmatic skills allow one to engage in conversations by taking turns, elaborating on a conversational topic, and changing topics appropriately. Behaviors such as making eye contact are also sometimes included in pragmatics.

In reviewing the language of males with fragile X syndrome, this chapter will address separately each of these three aspects of linguistic functioning. Issues involved in the specificity and development of fragile X speech and language also will be discussed, as will the limited data on linguistic functioning in carrier females.

SPEECH CHARACTERISTICS
OF FRAGILE X MALES

The early, informal terms used to describe peculiar speech characteristics in fragile X males (e.g., sing-songy, staccato) have now been replaced by formal research that describes problems in rate and impulsivity, repetitions of either parts of words or whole words, and articulation errors of various types.

A common research finding is that males with fragile X syndrome have difficulties involving the *rate and impulsivity* of speech. Many researchers note that fragile X speech is too fast, and that it is also unpredictable, with a mixture of short, rapid bursts of speech followed by long pauses. Wolf-Schein et al. (1987) noted that instances of dysrhythmia (uneven rate of speaking) occurred much more often in males with fragile X than in a suitably matched comparison group of Down syndrome children. Although further comparison work is needed, it may be that this speech pattern is characteristic of fragile X syndrome.

Other studies have identified IQ and age correlates of dysrhythmia. Hanson, Jackson, and Hagerman (1986) found fluctuating rates of speech in 9 of 10 subjects with IQs above 70. Borghgraef, Fryns, Dielkens, Pyck, and Van den Berghe (1987) found high rates of rapid speech rhythm and speech impulsiveness only among older fragile X boys aged 7 to 11 years, not in their younger subjects. In this older age group, speech problems were not related to IQ. Thus it may be that problems in the rate of speech are manifest in fragile X boys across the IQ spectrum, and that these problems become more pronounced with age.

Many researchers have also reported increased levels of *repetitions* of a part of a word or of an entire word in fragile X males. Newell, Sanborn, and Hagerman (1983), for example, found that 94% of their subjects showed either repetitions of a part-word ("R-r-rest") or whole word ("I-I-I get so tired"; from Newell et al., 1983, p. 182). Repetitions have even been noted in three Finnish-speaking children with fragile X syndrome (Vilkman, Niemi, & Ikonen, 1988).

Another speech problem involves either the *substitution or omission* of speech sounds, both in natural speech and in formal tests of articulation. Vowels and diphthongs (the *oi* in *boil* or the *ou* in *out*) are often misarticulated (Hanson et al., 1986), and virtually all reports note that males with fragile X syndrome more often make consonant substitutions, such as saying a *b* for *v* or *d* for *g* (Newell et al., 1983). This difficulty in articulating syllables is also demonstrated in tasks assessing "diadochokinesis" in which the child must repeat as quickly as possible clusters of the same consonant ("ba-ba-ba") versus those with different consonants ("pa-ta-ka"). Fragile X boys are able to perform the first task reasonably well, but they find the repetition of "non-reduplicative syllables," as in "pa-ta-ka" or words like *linoleum,* very difficult (Paul, Cohen, Breg, Watson, & Herman, 1984).

How can one understand these difficulties in rate, impulsivity, repetition, and articulation? Despite different emphases across investigators, most agree that such speech problems relate to difficulties in coordinating the complex oral-motor mechanisms involved in speaking. Although Paul et al. (1984) note the similarities of fragile X speech to the speech of children with verbal apraxia, Hanson et al. (1986) refer to these speech and articulation problems as "cluttering," a type of verbal clumsiness that is not as severe as and differs somewhat from stuttering. Regardless of the exact terminology used, males with fragile X display what Vilkman et al. (1988) refer to as "higher level motor encoding problems" (p. 218).

The possible presence of verbal apraxia, cluttering, or high-level motor encoding problems in males with fragile X syndrome also highlights the possible association of fragile X syndrome with short-term memory and attention deficits. Indeed, the inability to sequence syllables appropriately (as in diadochokinesis) is analogous to the difficulties that many of these males show on Sequential Processing tasks (see Chapter 4) and to their attentional problems (see Chapter 7). Difficulties in correctly sequencing behavior is one of the criteria of developmental apraxia of speech (Paul et al., 1984), just as attentional problems constitute one of the criteria for cluttering (Hanson et al., 1986). Although researchers thus focus on different speech problems in fragile X males, they all seem to involve deficits with attention and sequencing.

Syntax

Findings on the syntax or grammar of fragile X males are less well-described than their speech peculiarities. Several researchers have noted that levels of grammatical skills in fragile X males are consistent with their overall levels of intellectual functioning (e.g., Fryns, Jacobs, Kleczkowska, & Van den Berghe, 1984). In these studies, however, grammatical levels were determined in naturalistic speech samples, and only rough comparisons were made between these grammatical levels and overall intelligence.

In contrast, others have noted that males with fragile X syndrome have levels of grammar that fall below their skills in other areas. Weaknesses on several measures of grammar have been manifest by noninstitutionalized males (Marans et al., 1987), and deficits in expressive syntax have been shown by institutionalized fragile X males relative to nonspecific retarded subjects (Paul et al., 1987). Further, in a study of four families with X-linked mental retardation (only one of whom had fragile X), Howard-Peebles, Stoddard, and Mims (1979) observed that grammatical closure was a particular weakness for their subjects. Some researchers thus find that grammatical levels in fragile X males are comparable to their IQ or other skills, whereas other studies identify particular deficits in grammar.

In an effort to reconcile these contradictory findings, Sudhalter, Scarborough, and Cohen (1991) have recently assessed fragile X males across two grammatical measures: the child's mean (average) length of utterance (or MLU) and a newly devised measure of grammatical complexity, the Index of Productive Syntax (or IPSyn). They found that subjects showed comparable age-equivalent scores on these two measures. Sudhalter et al.

(1991) concluded that the grammar of males with fragile X syndrome is simply delayed in development "and thus attributable, in part, to their level of retardation" (p. 496).

Although these males were comparable on the two measures of grammar, it remains unclear whether these grammatical skills were comparable to overall intelligence or other linguistic skills. Indeed, comparing MLU and IPSyn age-scores of Sudhalter et al.'s (1991) subjects to their Communication age-scores on the Vineland Adaptive Behavior Scales (Sparrow, Balla, & Cicchetti, 1984), the mean age-scores of grammar (2.9 and 2.7 years by MLU and IPSyn, respectively) fall below the Vineland's Communication age-score of 4.9 years. For these males, then, it appears that grammar is an area of deficit—at least compared with overall communicative abilities. Until further study, however, it remains uncertain whether grammar in fragile X males is simply delayed or if it is a particular deficit relative to abilities in other areas.

Pragmatics

Research interest in pragmatics has stemmed, in part, from the findings that fragile X boys often show "autistic-like" behavior. Some researchers, therefore, have focused on perseveration with a particular word, phrase, or thought, and echolalia, or repeating the word or words of another. Poor eye contact is also occasionally noted in pragmatic studies; this feature is described in Chapter 7. Perseveration, echolalia, and poor eye contact are among the many symptoms that characterize autism in DSM-III-R and other diagnostic schemes. In addition to these autistic-like features, other aspects of pragmatics have also been examined in fragile X males, including conversational roles and inappropriate, deviant communication.

Conversational roles relate to the ability of the speaker to initiate, maintain, or appropriately change a conversational topic; to elicit new information; or to answer questions. Ferrier, Bashir, Meryash, Johnston, and Wolff (1991) compared 30-minute conversations of males with fragile X syndrome with age- and IQ-matched males with autism and with Down syndrome. Relative to their counterparts, fragile X males were more apt to engage in two types of conversational behaviors: "eliciting utterances," or questions, greetings, or requests for action; and "continuing utterances," or verbalizations that both respond to the previous utterance and elicit further conversation. Similarly, Sudhalter, Cohen, Silverman, and Wolf-Schein (1990) found that males with fragile X syndrome engaged in many more instances of conversational turn-taking compared with children with autism. These findings of better-developed conversational roles in fragile X males relative to other groups have implications for social relatedness issues discussed in Chapter 7.

Perseveration—on a word, phrase, or topic—has been a common finding in the speech of males with fragile X syndrome. All 10 of Hanson et al.'s (1986) subjects showed evidence of perseverative speech, and Borghgraef et al. (1987) noted perseverative speech in 62% of their 7- to 11-year-old boys. Males with fragile X syndrome show more perseverative speech than children with Down syndrome and nonspecific mental retardation (Reiss & Freund, 1992; Wolf-Schein et al., 1987). Sudhalter et al. (1990) have coined the term *deviant repetitive language* to characterize the perseverative language of males with fragile X syndrome. This term refers to a mixture of communicative types, including perseverations of phrases, sentences, or topics; jargon; and echolalia. In a comparative study, these researchers found that deviant repetitive language occurred most often in the autistic group, next most often in fragile X boys, and least often in Down syndrome subjects.

Inappropriate communication occurs when the child is truly off topic, or does not provide the listener with help or cues as to the meaning of the communication. Ferrier et al. (1991) found that relative to fragile X and Down syndrome children, autistic subjects provided the greatest number of inappropriate communications, including echolalia. Echolalia was also rarely present in Paul et al.'s (1987) study of older, institutionalized fragile X males, yet it was frequently encountered in their autistic subjects. Echolalia thus seems problematic for autistic subjects, whereas fragile X males are more apt to perseverate on phrases, sentences, or topics (Sudhalter et al., 1990).

Further differentiation of the conversational roles, perseveration, and inappropriate communications of fragile X males may be hampered by terminology. To Sudhalter et al. (1990), for example, the repetition of a word or phrase—as in "I can't, I can't"—constitutes an example of *deviant repetitive language*. To Newell et al. (1983), Ferrier et al. (1991), and others, this example would be a phrasal repetition or a partial repetition of self. Furthermore, the reasons for deviant repetitive language or word and phrasal repetitions are unclear. Repetitions may be symptomatic of motor encoding problems (e.g., Hanson et al., 1986), of pragmatic "deviance" (Sudhalter et al., 1990), or of "communicative placeholding" (Ferrier et al., 1991). It is also possible that both explanations are accurate: Difficulties in motor-encoding *and* pragmatic deviances may characterize the speech and language of males with fragile X syndrome.

ISSUES IN THE SPECIFICITY OF
FRAGILE X SPEECH AND LANGUAGE

Several researchers have addressed whether the speech-language features of males with fragile X syndrome are unique or shared with other mentally retarded groups, highlighting the need for appropriate contrast groups. Two widely used contrast groups have been persons with autism and persons with Down syndrome. Autistic groups have been helpful in differentiating between the pragmatic skills of fragile X and autistic males. In this regard, the more carefully conducted studies (e.g., Sudhalter et al., 1990) have only used fragile X males who are *not* diagnosed as autistic.

Persons with Down syndrome are a natural contrast group in that they have a relatively common and easily identified genetic disorder. It is critically important, however, to be aware that Down syndrome subjects have their own particular profiles of speech and language. Fowler (1990) has found that children with Down syndrome are particularly deficient in grammar compared with other areas of language (pragmatics, vocabulary). Individuals with Down syndrome, then, cannot be considered as stand-ins for "all persons with mental retardation"; as with many genetic disorders, these individuals also have their own, etiology-specific profiles of behavioral strengths and weaknesses (Hodapp & Dykens, 1992). Similarly, nonorganic mentally retarded individuals—up to 50%—may show deficits in expressive or receptive language (Miller & Chapman, 1984). Researchers thus need to be quite attuned to the limitations and assets imposed by various comparison groups. To control for either etiology-specific profiles or variations in nonorganic samples may require matching subjects across groups on certain speech-language variables, in addition to the usual matching variables of age, sex, and developmental level.

ISSUES IN THE DEVELOPMENT OF
LINGUISTIC FUNCTIONING

With few exceptions, a developmental framework has not yet been used to examine the language of individuals with fragile X syndrome. Based on other domains of behavioral functioning, however, it may be that linguistic profiles and rates of development differ across various ages. This hypothesis stems from studies of intellectual and adaptive functioning that show males with fragile X slow in their development beginning at or near the pubertal years (see Chapters 4 and 6). Early adolescence may also be the time when intellectual and adaptive strengths and weaknesses become more pronounced (Dykens, Hodapp, Ort, & Leckman, 1992; Hodapp et al., 1991) and when there are shifts in certain brain structures (Reiss, 1992). Preliminary evidence suggests that certain language characteristics may indeed change as boys with fragile X syndrome develop. Borghgraef et al. (1987) found that only older fragile X boys, aged 7 to 11 years, had difficulties with speech rhythm or impulsivity; younger boys, aged 2 to 7, did not manifest these problems. Although these findings are only suggestive, they highlight the need for a developmental perspective on the speech and language functioning of males with fragile X syndrome.

SPEECH-LANGUAGE CHARACTERISTICS OF FEMALES WITH FRAGILE X SYNDROME

To date, there is only one study on the speech and language of females with fragile X syndrome. In a study of 12 members of an extended family, Madison, George, and Moeschler (1986) examined the speech and language characteristics of six females ranging in age from 6 to 63 years. Two of the five adult women were of low-average intelligence, the remaining three showed moderate, mild, and borderline intelligence. There was also a 6-year-old girl, who was severely mentally retarded.

Although the expressive and receptive vocabularies of these six females were equally developed, Madison et al. (1986) noted several idiosyncracies in speech and pragmatics. Specifically, the speech of these women was considered to be clear and intelligible, although all five women performed diadochokinetic tasks especially slowly. The speech of each woman featured revisions (self-corrections) on a high percentage—up to 20%—of their phrases. Each of the adults also repeated automatic phrases such as "of course," "well," and "special."

Pragmatically, Madison et al. (1986) noted that, "Among the three lower-functioning women, appropriateness of speech content was inconsistent, particularly in the type and amount of information given" (p. 139). The conversations of all five adults were characterized by a "detailed, run-on narrative style." These findings of speech and pragmatic idiosyncracies are in need of further study with larger numbers of females, especially as they seem consistent with problems in social relatedness found in some carrier females (see Chapter 7).

SUMMARY

Since Lehrke's initial observations of speech problems in fragile X males, research has identified consistent problems in speech (e.g., rate and impulsivity, repetitions, substitutions and omissions) and pragmatics (e.g., perseveration) that may be unique to males with this disorder. Why such differences occur remains unknown, with possible explanations including motor-encoding difficulties and ties to autism or autistic-like behaviors.

There is a need for further research with fragile X males that identifies the course of their linguistic development, especially throughout those time periods (prepubertal and pubertal) when shifts in cognitive functioning are apt to occur. In addition, research needs to identify the specificity of speech and language features of fragile X males with appropriately matched comparison groups. Finally, studies are needed that describe the speech and language characteristics of affected carrier females and that relate these features to problems in social relatedness and thinking that are manifest by some of these women.

6

ADAPTIVE FUNCTIONING

The ability of mentally retarded persons to be socially competent—to adapt to various personal and social demands—is a critical component of their long-term adjustment and overall success in life. Social adaptation may be even more important than IQ in determining the ultimate success of mentally retarded persons living either in the community or in an institutional setting (e.g., Landesman-Dwyer & Sulzbacher, 1981). Not surprisingly, adaptive behavior has long played a role in the definition of mental retardation. Indeed, beginning with the 1983 manual of the American Association on Mental Retardation (AAMR; Grossman, 1983), equal importance has been given to deficits in intelligence *and* adaptive behavior in definitions of mental retardation. The recently revised, 1992 AAMR definition of mental retardation specifies these adaptive behavior deficits even further. According to the revised AAMR manual, mental retardation "is characterized by significantly subaverage intellectual functioning, existing concurrently with related limitations in two or more of the following applicable adaptive skills: communication, self-care, home living, social skills, community use, self-direction, health and safety, functional academics, leisure, and work" (Luckasson et al., 1992, p. 5).

Although the importance of adaptive behavior has thus been well established, there are only a handful of studies on the social adaptation of individuals with fragile X syndrome. This de-emphasis on adaptive behavior is seen also in the larger field of mental retardation and has been attributed, in part, to problems in defining and measuring social adaptation (Zigler, Balla, & Hodapp, 1984).

THE CONSTRUCT
OF ADAPTIVE BEHAVIOR

What, then, is adaptive behavior? Doll (1953), the first to emphasize and measure this construct in mentally retarded persons, defined adaptive behavior as "the functional ability of the human organism for exercising personal independence and social responsibility" (p. 10). Doll, who was affiliated with the Vineland Training School in Vineland, NJ, operationalized this construct in the Vineland Social Maturity Scale. Since Doll's contributions, many other definitions and measurements of adaptive behavior have been developed, and most share at least four assumptions.

The first common assumption is that adaptive behavior is a *developmental construct;* that is, what is considered adaptive necessarily changes as children develop. The adaptive behavior expectations for preschool children differ from the social and personal demands of adolescence or young adulthood.

Second, adaptive behavior is an inherently *social construct*; it is defined by others' expectations and thus by one's larger society or culture. How and when an adolescent adapts to the demands of inner-city life in the United States presumably differs from the expectations of adolescents in rural Guatemala.

Third, the performance of adaptive behavior may *differ across various situations*. A child may, for example, show below-average achievement, IQ, and adaptive skills in school, but adequate social adaptation in other settings—the so-called 6-hour retarded child that has created much controversy in the mental retardation field. As such, it is important to assess adaptive skills across the multiple settings that people find themselves in, such as school, work, home, and community.

Finally, adaptive behavior is measured by *typical as opposed to optimal performance*. Unlike intelligence testing, in which the examiner strives for optimal testing conditions that facilitate the subject's best performance, assessing adaptive skills depends on those behaviors that a person typically or habitually exhibits throughout the course of everyday living. Thus if a child can perform certain behaviors but does not typically do so (for any number of reasons), he or she, by definition, has compromised adaptive functioning.

Measurements of adaptive behavior, then, must reflect these four features: They need to have a developmental orientation; be culturally sensitive; examine behavior across multiple settings; and assess typical performance, not capability. Unlike earlier years, there are now many available instruments that assess adaptive skills. These instruments vary considerably in how well they have been standardized or normed and in the age ranges and specific domains of adaptive skills that they assess. To date, most studies on the adaptive functioning of fragile X males have used the recently revised Vineland Adaptive Behavior Scales (Sparrow et al., 1984). The Vineland scales were adapted from Doll's (1965) original Vineland Social Maturity Scale and are sensitive to the four features described above. Administered in a semi-structured interview format to the subject's primary caregiver, the Vineland assesses "the performance of daily activities required for personal and social sufficiency" (Sparrow et al., 1984, p. 6). The Vineland consists of four domains and 11 subdomains: Communication (with subdomains of expressive, receptive, and written communication); Daily Living Skills (personal, domestic, community); Socialization (interpersonal relationships, coping skills, play and leisure time); and Motor Skills (fine and gross).

ADAPTIVE FUNCTIONING IN
FRAGILE X SYNDROME

Profiles of Adaptive Functioning

Studies of mixed etiological groups have generally not found profiles of adaptive strength or weakness (e.g., Sparrow et al., 1984). In contrast, however, studies that assess adaptive functioning within particular etiological groups have discovered specific adaptive strengths and weaknesses. Subjects with Down syndrome, for example, often show adaptive weaknesses in communication, especially in expressive skills relative to receptive abilities (e.g., Dykens, Hodapp, & Evans, 1992). Individuals with Prader-Willi syndrome have adaptive strengths in daily living skills, especially in domestic skills, and weaknesses in socialization, particularly coping skills (Dykens, Hodapp, Walsh, & Nash, 1992a).

In fragile X syndrome as well, specific profiles of adaptive functioning have been reported. Wolff, Gardner, Lappen, Paccia, and Schnell (1987) noted strengths in daily living skills in their fragile X sample, yet they did not take the institutional status of their subjects into account. In a study that separately examined 12 older, institutionalized men and 15 younger, noninstitutionalized fragile X boys, Dykens, Hodapp, and Leckman (1989) found that both groups showed strengths in Daily Living Skills relative to the Communication and Socialization domains of the Vineland scales. Within Daily Living Skills itself, these subjects showed particular strengths in domestic and personal skills (e.g., household chores and grooming). Adaptive strengths in Daily Living Skills were thus evident in fragile X males regardless of their living setting and across a wide age range, from 3 to 51 years. More recent studies suggest that relative strengths in Daily Living Skills may become even more pronounced with advancing age (Dykens, Hodapp, Ort, & Leckman, 1993; Weigers, 1992). These adaptive strengths have been confirmed in studies that directly compared fragile X males with suitably matched control subjects. Dykens, Leckman, Paul, and Watson (1988) found that institutionalized fragile X subjects showed strengths in domestic Daily Living Skills relative to their autistic and nonspecific mentally retarded counterparts. These fragile X males also had levels of domestic and personal skills that far exceeded mental age expectations. Comparing noninstitutionalized fragile X and Down syndrome boys matched on age and overall level of adaptive functioning, Dykens, Hodapp, Ort, and Leckman (1992) found strengths in Daily Living skills only among fragile X males, and weaknesses in expressive communication only in Down syndrome boys.

Although these comparative studies suggest possible specificity of the fragile X adaptive profile, additional data are needed that directly compare fragile X males with other etiologic and nonspecific mentally retarded groups. This research is particularly important as other etiologic groups may also show strengths in daily living skills. Persons with Prader-Willi syndrome, for example, have relative strengths in this domain, yet they also seem to have areas of adaptive weakness that are not necessarily shared by fragile X males (Dykens et al., 1992a).

There is also a pressing need for studies on the adaptive features of fragile X females. No data are yet available on the adaptive profiles of affected versus unaffected carrier girls and women. Like males, it may be that these females show strengths in daily living skills. Unlike males, some of these affected females may show more pronounced, relative weaknesses in socialization skills due to difficulties that they have with many aspects of relating to others (see Chapter 7). At present, these hypotheses remain unexplored.

Relationship Between IQ and Adaptive Behavior in Fragile X Syndrome

The relationship between intelligence and adaptive behavior is somewhat controversial in the larger mental retardation field. Some researchers emphasize the importance of IQ in defining mental retardation (e.g.,

Zigler et al., 1984), whereas others consider social adaptation as mental retardation's central defining characteristic (e.g., Barnett, 1986).

Such debates generally consider intelligence and adaptive functioning as unrelated; that the two are theoretically different and are also measured in different ways. As such, one would not expect IQ and adaptive behavior to be highly related. Indeed, only low to moderate correlations between IQ and adaptive behavior have been found among mentally retarded groups of mixed and unknown etiologies (Sparrow et al., 1984). Among fragile X males, however, there appears to be a significant relationship between intelligence and adaptive behavior. Dykens, Hodapp, Ort, and Leckman (1992) found significant correlations between mental age and age-equivalent scores on the Vineland scales in noninstitutionalized fragile X males. Further, mental age in these males was correlated about equally across the Vineland's three domains. Similarly, Dykens et al. (1988) observed that institutionalized men with fragile X syndrome, aged 23 to 51, had levels of adaptive behavior that were generally commensurate with, or that exceeded, their mental ages.

Unlike studies of mixed or unknown etiologies, these data suggest that there may be a relationship between intelligence and adaptive behavior in fragile X syndrome, as well as in other specific etiological groups. Indeed, significant correlations between IQ and adaptive behavior have also been found in Prader-Willi syndrome (Dykens et al., 1992a) and in Down syndrome (Loveland & Kelly, 1988). Collectively, these studies underscore the importance of separately examining specific etiological groups.

It may be that intelligence sets an upper limit or ceiling to adaptive accomplishments, thereby resolving some of the controversy in the field as to the relative importance of these two constructs. If so, this limit may be more pronounced at lower levels of intelligence. This type of finding was observed in a 40-year follow-up study of special education students (Ross et al., 1985). This study found that severely and profoundly retarded adults were rarely self-sufficient, while the outcomes of students with mild mental retardation were quite variable—some were completely to partly self-sufficient, while others were "dependent."

If similar findings were to hold for fragile X syndrome, one would expect to find high correlations between IQ and adaptive behavior standard scores among lower functioning males, and more variability (and lower correlations) between IQ and adaptive functioning in higher functioning individuals. In fragile X syndrome, the significant correlations between IQ and adaptation found thus far have been in males who typically had moderate mental retardation. Future research needs to identify the relationship between IQ and adaptive behavior in low versus high functioning fragile X males; this relationship could also be assessed in fragile X females who are either affected or unaffected carriers.

Trajectory of Adaptive Behavior

The development of adaptive behavior in mentally retarded persons in general has received considerable attention. Some studies have identified gains in the overall adaptive levels of noninstitutionalized mentally retarded persons until about age 15, at which point a developmental plateau is reached (Eyman & Arndt, 1982). Other studies, however, suggest better-developed adaptive skills in older versus middle-aged mentally retarded adults (e.g., Krauss & Seltzer, 1986), indicating improved adaptive functioning in the later years.

Various domains of adaptive functioning may have different trajectories, and these variable courses have been shown to differ according to living setting and level of cognitive impairment (e.g., Widaman, Borthwick-Duffy, & Little, 1991). Widaman et al. (1991), for example, found that unlike severely and profoundly retarded individuals, higher-functioning subjects showed gains in certain daily living skills throughout adolescence. Higher-functioning individuals also sustained these gains until their 60s, whereas lower-functioning subjects showed earlier declines in these skills. The trajectory of adaptive skills thus seems influenced by IQ, institutional status, and the types of adaptive skills being assessed.

In addition to these features, research suggests that the trajectory of adaptive behavior also may vary according to etiological group. The adaptive trajectories of persons with Down syndrome have been studied quite extensively due to the association between aging and evidence of Alzheimer's disease in this syndrome. Some studies have found declines in the adaptive functioning of persons with Down syndrome: These declines are pronounced in subjects aged 50 and older, particularly in the domain of motor skills (e.g., Brown, Greer, Aylward, & Hunt, 1990). It may be, however, that these declines are not unique to Down syndrome. Silverstein et al. (1988) found no differences between the age-related adaptive declines shown by Down syndrome and suitably matched control subjects. The extent to which adaptive declines in Down syndrome are shared among other groups or are different across various domains thus remains unclear.

In striking contrast to Down syndrome, very little is known about the trajectory of adaptive behavior in males with fragile X syndrome. The need to study adaptive development in fragile X syndrome is underscored by recent findings regarding the cognitive trajectory of these males. Briefly, many fragile X males show steady growth in mental age until the 10- to 15-year period, at which point IQ declines and mental age plateaus (see Chapter 4). Given the correlation between IQ and adaptive functioning found in fragile X males, it may be that their adaptive behavior follows a similar path of development as their cognitive functioning.

In a preliminary study, Dykens et al. (1993) assessed adaptive behavior in 17 fragile X males aged 1 to 17 on two occasions that were at least 1 year apart. Using the Vineland scales, these researchers found that younger subjects, aged 1 to 10, showed increases in overall adaptive behavior scores, as well as in Vineland Communication, Daily Living Skills, and Socialization domains. Older subjects, aged 10 through 17, however, manifested consistent declines from first to second testing in overall Vineland scores and in each of the three domains. Despite these declines, older subjects showed a more pronounced pattern of adaptive strengths in Daily Living Skills relative to the younger groups.

Although this study suggests an age-related decline in adaptive functioning that may parallel well-established declines in IQ, findings should be considered preliminary to further efforts. There is a need to examine this issue with larger numbers of fragile X males across a wider age range and to compare these findings with appropriate control groups. In a study of eight institutionalized fragile X males and matched controls, Curfs, Schreppers-Tijdink, Wiegers, van Velzen, and Fryns (1989) found a similar course of development in both groups. Although these comparable trajectories may be associated with the effects of institutionalization, this study does point up the need for appropriate comparison groups. Further studies also are needed that document the course of adaptive development in affected and unaffected fragile X females.

SUMMARY

The importance of adaptive behavior in the success of mentally retarded persons has been well established, and these skills have long played a role in the definition of mental retardation. Yet data are fairly limited on the adaptive features of fragile X males. The specificity of the fragile X profile of relative strengths in daily living skills (especially personal and domestic skills) needs to be tested in further comparisons with other etiological and nonspecific groups. The parallels between declines in IQ and adaptive behavior also require further comparative study. In addition, adaptive functioning in affected and unaffected females remains unknown. Although the relative importance of intelligence versus adaptation continues to be debated, few would disagree that adaptive skills are critical in optimizing the functioning of mentally retarded persons. But many parents report that features other than intelligence seem to be impeding their child's optimal adaptation. Specifically, many fragile X males can perform adaptive skills that are consistent with, or exceed, their mental ages, but they may not do so because they are not in the "right mood," are "too hyper," or have a "short attention span." These so-called maladaptive behaviors—discussed in the next chapter—may thus hinder optimal adaptive functioning in many persons with fragile X syndrome.

7

PSYCHOPATHOLOGY AND MALADAPTIVE BEHAVIOR

Psychopathology and maladaptive behavior have been highly researched in fragile X syndrome. More than 100 studies have identified whether persons with fragile X syndrome show higher-than-usual prevalence rates for autism, attention deficits, hyperactivity, social anxiety, and other disorders. More recently, the psychological problems of carrier females also have been a focus of research.

Some of the interest in psychopathology in fragile X syndrome may stem from the field of dual diagnosis—or diagnosing persons with both mental retardation and psychiatric disorder. Research in dual diagnosis has established that persons with mental retardation may show a variety of psychiatric problems, including schizophrenia, depression, and anxiety and personality disorders. Factors such as age, sex, IQ, and living setting influence both the types and prevalence rates of psychiatric problems in mentally retarded persons (e.g., Jacobson, 1990).

In all of this work, however, researchers have yet to consider how etiology—the cause of a person's mental retardation—affects the expression of psychiatric problems. This inattention to etiology, including genetic disorders, is a common research bias in both dual diagnosis and in the mental retardation field (Hodapp & Dykens, in press). Yet it does appear that individuals with fragile X syndrome share a predisposition to specific types of psychopathology (Bregman, Leckman, & Ort, 1988). Fragile X syndrome is now associated with a range of psychiatric problems in both males and females, including autism, pervasive developmental disorder, attention deficit hyperactivity disorder, anxiety disorder, schizotypal disorder, and depression. Some people with fragile X syndrome also have seizure disorders, and a handful of individuals may have Tourette's syndrome, sleep apnea, and Klinefelter's syndrome. This chapter describes each of these disorders and behavior problems in both affected males and carrier females.

THE AUTISM CONTROVERSY

Although many conditions co-occur with fragile X syndrome, the association of fragile X syndrome and autism has been the most captivating to researchers. This absorption seems due, in part, to early suggestions that fragile X syndrome could be a frequently occurring genetic "cause" of autism. The links between fragile X syndrome and autism have generated considerable controversy, and these debates have led to more refined research questions. Yet the autism controversy has also pulled research attention away from other psychiatric and behavioral problems in fragile X syndrome, including problems such as impulsivity and anxiety that are more prevalent than autism per se.

Early work on the fragile X-autism connection, conducted primarily in the 1980s, assessed if there was an increased prevalence rate of autistic disorder in males with fragile X syndrome. This research used two methods: Autistic samples were screened to identify the presence of the fragile X marker, and fragile X samples were examined for autistic disorder. A high prevalence rate in either case would suggest a strong association between the two disorders. More recent research, however, has de-emphasized these diagnostic issues and instead focused on refined descriptions of the many autistic-like behaviors found in fragile X males. After reviewing the earlier prevalence studies, this chapter identifies how recent behavioral research has shed new light on the autism controversy.

Prevalence of Fragile X Syndrome
Among Autistic Samples

In the early 1980s, three autistic, mentally retarded boys with fragile X syndrome were described by two research groups (August & Lockhart, 1984; Meryash, Szymanski, & Gerald, 1982). These young boys manifested deviant or delayed language, stereotypical and ritualistic behaviors, poor and fleeting eye contact, and impaired social relationships.

These early case reports suggested that fragile X syndrome may account for some of the 4 to 1 predominance of males with autism, perhaps forming a distinct subgroup within autism (August & Lockhart, 1984). The prevalence of these newly identified cases was unclear, with sugges-

TABLE 7.1 Studies That Screened Autistic Subjects for Fragile X Syndrome

Researchers	Number of Autistic Subjects	Percentage of Subjects With Fragile X Syndrome
Watson et al., 1984	76	5.3
Venter et al., 1984	40	0
Jorgensen et al., 1984	23	4
Goldfine et al., 1985	37	0
Blomquist et al., 1985	102	16
Pueschel et al., 1985	18	0
McGillivray et al., 1986	33	9
Wright et al., 1986	40	2.5
Wahlstrom et al., 1986	143	13
Fisch et al., 1986	144	12.5
Brown et al., 1986	183	13.1
Payton et al., 1989	85	2.4
Wahlstrom et al., 1989	52	9
Ho & Kalousek, 1989	45	2
Cantu et al., 1990	67	1
Tranebjaerg & Kure, 1991	32	6

tions that they could be either "coincidental" (Meryash et al., 1982, p. 299) or of a "significant frequency" (Brown et al., 1982, p. 307). As such, these early reports called for studies that screened larger samples of autistic males for the fragile X marker.

Considerable excitement was generated by the possibility that fragile X syndrome might be a genetic cause of autism. As a result, the initial case reports were followed by a flurry of research—more than 20 studies—that screened variable numbers of autistic individuals for fragile X syndrome. These autistic subjects also varied in age, institutional status, and degree of intellectual impairment. As summarized in Table 7.1, prevalence rates for fragile X syndrome among these autistic samples ranged from 0 to 16%, with a mode of about 4% to 5%.

This wide variability in prevalence rates has been attributed to several sources of error. First, given the relatively low co-occurrence of fragile X syndrome and autism, rates are likely to be affected by the size of the sample studied. Table 7.1 reveals that sample sizes ranged from 18 to 183 subjects. In a review of 15 prevalence studies, Fisch, Cohen, Jenkins, and Brown (1988) determined that negative results (no fragile X cases) were associated with studies using small samples. In contrast, studies with 100 or more subjects yielded comparable prevalence rates of 13% to 16%.

Because the studies in Table 7.1 screened subjects with previously established diagnoses of autism, variability in prevalence also may be attributed to the lack of uniformly applied a priori diagnostic criteria for autism. These studies may also have been susceptible to ascertainment bias—a reliance on clinic subjects who generally have more severe problems relative to a community or nonreferred sample.

Despite errors associated with sample size and diagnostic ambiguities, some researchers have asserted that fragile X is a common genetic marker in autism, accounting for 15% to 20% of autistic males (e.g., Blomquist et al., 1985; Brown et al., 1986). Others have opposed this view, claiming that fragile X may account for just 3% of autistic males (e.g., Goldfine et al., 1985; Payton, Steele, Wenger, & Minshew, 1989; Wright, Young, Edwards, Abramson, & Duncan, 1986).

Central to these opposing conclusions are arguments that compare differential prevalence rates of fragile X syndrome in autism versus in mental retardation in general. Blomquist et al. (1985) and Gillberg and Wahlstrom (1985) assert that their rates of fragile X and autism—16% to 20%—far exceed percentages of retarded males with fragile X syndrome. As such, these researchers conclude that fragile X syndrome is more strongly associated with autism than with mentally retarded males.

In contrast to these researchers, Watson et al. (1984) and Payton, Steele, Wenger, and Minshew (1989) have claimed that their prevalence rates of autism and fragile X (3% and 5.3%, respectively) are no higher than the rate of fragile X syndrome among mentally retarded males. Fragile X syndrome should not, then, increase the "risk of autism above that consequent to mental retardation itself" (Payton et al., 1989, p. 417).

In support of this latter position, Einfeld, Molony, and Hall (1989) have asserted that links between fragile X syndrome and autism may exist only because both disorders are associated with mental retardation. To test this hypothesis, they compared autistic symptomatology in 45 fragile X and 45 non-fragile X males who were matched on age and IQ.

Controlling for ascertainment bias, Einfeld et al. (1989) found comparable rates of autism in both groups as assessed by DSM-III-R (American Psychiatric Association [APA], 1987) criteria and two checklists of autistic behavior. Fragile X males exhibited more hand flapping and gaze avoidance than control subjects. Gaze avoidance was found to decline with age and as subjects became less shy and more familiar with the researchers. Hall and Einfeld (1990) point out that these behavioral shifts are inconsistent with the persistent aloofness and indifference of autism, and that the initial presence of these symptoms in subjects may have "misled" previous researchers into making an autistic diagnosis. Comparable rates of autism were thus found in fragile X and non-fragile X groups in Einfeld et al.'s (1989) well-controlled study. A recent review of 58 prevalence studies by Fisch (1992) adds further support to comparable rates of autism in fragile X and non-fragile X males. Fisch (1992) found virtually identical pooled proportions of fragile X syndrome in autistic males and in mentally retarded males in general: 5.4% and 5.5%, respectively.

From studies of autistic individuals, then, it seems that autism and fragile X do indeed co-occur, but that the prevalence of these cases is much lower than originally thought, approximately 3% to 5% (Fisch, 1992; Payton et al., 1989; Rutter et al., 1990; Watson et al., 1984). Inflated estimates in many studies are attributable to ascertainment bias; diverse sample sizes; and nonstandard procedures for making a priori diagnoses of autism, which may have included an overreliance on easily identified behaviors such as hand flapping and gaze avoidance.

It is also clear that fragile X syndrome is one of many genetic disorders associated with autism (e.g., Rett syndrome, Cri-du-chat syndrome, Cornelia de Lange syndrome, PKU, tuberous sclerosis). Given the large number of individuals with fragile X syndrome, however, it may be the leading hereditary disorder that co-occurs with autism.

Prevalence of Autism Among Fragile X Males

A second approach to the autism controversy turns the search around by assessing how many fragile X males may be diagnosed with autism. As shown in Table 7.2, the prevalence rates of autism among fragile X males vary even more widely than in the previous analyses, from 5% to 60%. Table 7.2 also reveals that sample sizes in these studies range from 9 to 150 males. Similar to studies of fragile X in autism, variability in rates of autism among fragile X males may be attributed to sample size and ascertainment bias (Brown et al., 1986).

An additional—and striking—source of error in these studies is the lack of uniform diagnostic criteria for autism. As indicated in Table 7.2, diagnostic criteria were often not reported, and even when used, criteria ranged from systematic approaches to informal methods. Such diverse diagnostic procedures can lead to widely different rates of autism. Indeed, Hagerman, Jackson, Levitas, Rimland, and Braden (1986) found that 46%

TABLE 7.2 Studies of Autism in Fragile X Subjects

Researchers	Number of Fragile X Males	Percentage of Subjects With Autism	Diagnostic Criteria for Autism
Brown et al., 1982	22	23	Rutter
Fryns & Van den Berghe, 1983	30	16	Not stated
Jacobs et al., 1983	9	22	Not stated
Levitas et al., 1983	10	60	DSM-III
Nielsen, 1983	27	33	4 behaviors
Fryns et al., 1984	21	14	2 behaviors
Partington, 1984	61	5	3 behaviors
Rhoads, 1984	17	18	Not stated
Benezech & Noel, 1985	28	53	DSM-III
Brown et al., 1986	150	17	DSM-III
Hagerman, Jackson et al., 1986	50	46	DSM-III
Borghgraef et al., 1987	23	39	Autiscale
Bregman et al., 1988	14	7	DSM-III
Reiss & Freund, 1990	17	18	DSM-III-R

of their fragile X sample met criteria for autism using DSM-III; 30% did so using the Autism Behavior Checklist; and none did so using a strict, Kannerian definition of autism.

The extremely wide range of prevalence rates in Table 7.2 may also reflect differences of opinion among clinicians and researchers regarding the primary deficit in autism. Some emphasize the lack of attachment to caregivers and other social deficits as the hallmark of autism (e.g., Volkmar, 1987), while others view deviant nonverbal communication and language (e.g., Paul, 1987) or cognitive and perceptual abnormalities (e.g., Frith & Baron-Cohen, 1987) as central to the disorder. Reiss and Freund (1992) suggest that these individual biases interact with the lack of specificity in DSM-III-R criteria (e.g., patients need to meet 8 out of 16 criteria) to foster variability in rates of autism in fragile X males.

Individual biases and variability in diagnostic criteria across research groups emphasize the need for researchers at least to be consistent among themselves in using their diagnostic procedures, whatever those procedures might be. Inter-rater reliabilities in making diagnoses of autism, however, were only reported in 2 of the 14 studies in Table 7.2 (Bregman et al., 1988; Reiss & Freund, 1990). Nonstandard diagnostic procedures across studies and unknown reliabilities within studies both contribute to variable rates of autism among fragile X males.

Toward a More Behavioral Focus
on Autistic-Like Features

As the fragile X-autism prevalence studies have had multiple methodological problems, the time seems long overdue to shift research attention away from prevalence or diagnostic issues. Instead, considerable light could be shed on the autism controversy by research that provides fine-tuned descriptions of autistic-like behaviors in fragile X males. These fine-tuned analyses may ultimately identify behaviors that are uniquely characteristic of fragile X syndrome, independent from autism.

As suggested by the case of Jason in Chapter 1, many males with fragile X syndrome—up to 90%—exhibit various combinations of autistic behaviors and traits (Hagerman, Jackson et al., 1986). These autistic features have been clarified recently in a comparative study of fragile X and developmentally delayed boys matched on age and IQ. Using DSM-III-R criteria for autism, Reiss and Freund (1992) found that the two groups were similar in their attachment behaviors with caregivers (e.g., comfort seeking, affective awareness, imitation). The two groups also differed in many ways. Relative to controls, fragile X boys exhibited more dysfunctional play with peers; repetitive motor behaviors, such as rocking and hand flapping; hand biting; and impaired verbal and nonverbal communication, such as perseverations and gaze aversion. Further, abnormalities in perceiving sensory stimuli, including overreactions to sound or smelling and mouthing objects, were also seen in many fragile X subjects.

Many of these autistic behaviors are prominent in younger males and may decrease in frequency or severity with advancing age (Borghgraef et al., 1987; Reiss & Freund, 1990). In particular, with increasing age many fragile X males become more responsive to others, show less perseverative speech, and show less exaggerated responses to environmental change (Borghgraef et al., 1987; Hagerman, Jackson et al., 1986; Reiss & Freund, 1990).

Some studies suggest that the severity of autistic behaviors decreases as IQ increases (Borghgraef et al., 1987; Levitas et al., 1983). In contrast, others find that the severity of autistic behaviors is not related to IQ, and that males with severe autistic behaviors are found across the IQ spectrum (Gillberg, Persson, & Wahlstom, 1986; Reiss & Freund, 1990).

Some of the autistic behaviors noted by Reiss and Freund (1992) and other researchers have recently been examined in an in-depth manner; specifically, gaze aversion; problems in social relatedness; and perseverative, echolalic speech. Chapter 5 addresses abnormalities in speech and language, and findings to date on the remaining two behaviors—gaze and relatedness problems—point to both similarities and discontinuities with autism. As such, these in-depth studies offer preliminary evidence for a unique fragile X behavioral phenotype.

Gaze Aversion. Individuals with fragile X syndrome and those with autism both manifest poor eye contact, yet they seem to differ in certain aspects of this difficulty. In a series of studies, Cohen, Vietze, Sudhalter, Jenkins, and Brown (1989, 1991) analyzed gaze aversion in non-autistic and autistic fragile X males relative to suitably matched subjects with autism. Mutual eye contact was aversive to many fragile X males regardless of their age or communicative ability (Cohen, Vietze et al., 1991). In contrast, autistic individuals showed more responsive eye contact with advancing age and with increasing communicative abilities.

Unlike their autistic counterparts, fragile X males were found to be sensitive to parent-initiated social gaze, but mutual eye contact was aversive to them (Cohen et al., 1989). Fragile X males avoided mutual gaze by not looking at their parents when their parents looked at them, waiting for their parents to look elsewhere, and then returning the gaze. Both non-autistic and autistic fragile X males were thus more attuned and responsive to parental social cues than autistic subjects; findings that have different implications for the deficits in social relatedness seen in each of these groups.

Social Relatedness, Avoidance, and Anxiety. Eye contact is a central part of communicating with others, and as such, the gaze aversion that characterizes so many fragile X males is intimately related to their problems in social interaction. Superficial descriptions of the social interactions of fragile X males seem inconsistent, ranging from a friendly, pleasant, and comfortable stance (Levitas et al., 1983), to a shy and anxious style with others (Nielsen, 1983).

This simultaneously shy but friendly presentation is succinctly demonstrated in the so-called fragile X handshake. As described by Wolff, Gardner, Paccia, and Lappen (1989), this handshake consists of a well-coordinated response in which fragile X males take another's hand, but turn their head and upper trunk to avert mutual eye gaze, and then mumble a conventional social greeting. Wolff et al. (1989) found that this handshake persisted over time with both strangers and parents and was unique to fragile X males relative to matched Down syndrome controls. The fragile X handshake thus seems to reflect a simultaneous willingness to interact and a strong element of social avoidance.

Recent research supports a high level of socially avoidant behaviors in many fragile X males. Cohen et al. (1988) found that fragile X males showed high levels of socially avoidant behaviors with both parents and strangers relative to Down syndrome and normal controls. These avoidant behaviors included turning away from others or from others' task expectations. Unlike subjects with autism, however, fragile X males were more socially avoidant of strangers compared with their parents. Fragile X males thus showed a level of wariness to strangers not exhibited by their less discriminating autistic counterparts.

Other researchers have described excessive shyness and socially related anxieties in their fragile X samples (e.g., Bregman et al., 1988; Einfeld, 1988; Nielsen, 1983). Bregman et al. (1988) report that social anxieties were manifest in self-consciousness among their fragile X subjects, as well as in worries regarding performance, competence, and acceptability. Using DSM-III criteria, these researchers found that more than a third of their sample met criteria for avoidant, overanxious, and generalized anxiety disorders.

Fragile X males may, however, become less shy and anxious—and more friendly, cooperative, and sociable—when "comfortable" with their examiners (e.g., Rhoads, 1984) or "more familiar" with them (Einfeld et al., 1989). These features contrast with the persistent aloofness and social indifference that are the hallmarks of autism.

Unlike autistic individuals, then, most fragile X males relate well to others, including their parents, and only a few show the profound indifference characteristic of autism. Fragile X individuals may therefore be placed on a spectrum of socially avoidant behavior that ranges in severity from autism at one extreme to shyness at the other extreme. Although social avoidance, anxieties, and gaze aversion are particularly heightened with strangers, these features seem to dissipate with increasing familiarity. These behaviors do not, however, remit completely and are quite evident even in interactions with familiar people. It may be that fragile X males evidence more persistent problems in social relatedness with peers than with their caregivers (Reiss & Freund, 1990, 1992)—a finding in need of further study. The mechanisms underlying this socially avoidant spectrum remain unknown. It may be that the region of the fragile X marker is associated with social dominance and with the fragile site inducing abnormalities in dominance, such as avoidance, gaze aversion, the fragile

X handshake, and tactile defensiveness (Cohen, Sudhalter et al., 1991). Some of the avoidant and autistic behaviors in fragile X syndrome also may be associated with similarities in the posterior fossa (brain structures related to involuntary functions, such as movement and coordination) that have been observed across a small number of autistic and fragile X subjects (Reiss, Aylward, Freund, Joshi, & Bryan, 1991).

Pervasive Developmental Disorder (PDD)

Many fragile X males have oddities in social relatedness that may be captured by a diagnosis of pervasive developmental disorder, or PDD. As outlined by DSM-III (APA 1980), PDD includes many behaviors commonly shown by fragile X males, such as motor stereotypes, perseverative speech, preoccupations with particular objects or subjects (e.g., vacuum cleaners, the *Wizard of Oz*), self-abuse, temper tantrums, and hypersensitivities to sensory stimuli. The DSM-III-R (APA, 1987), however, offers no such criteria for PDD. Instead, these features are characterized as "not otherwise specified," or PDD-NOS.

To approximate a PDD-NOS diagnosis, Reiss and Freund (1990) adapted DSM-III-R autism criteria by reducing requirements for the numbers of symptoms. Using this definition, they found that 41% of their sample of 17 fragile X males met "criteria" for PDD-NOS. This diagnostic proxy, however, may not capture qualitative differences between autism and pervasive developmental disorder. A more accurate approach would be to develop specific diagnostic criteria for PDD-NOS (e.g., Towbin, Dykens, Pearson, & Cohen, 1993) and apply these criteria to fragile X individuals.

Thought disorder is often found to varying degrees in PDD-NOS, and it is also manifest by high-functioning autistic subjects (Dykens, Volkmar, & Glick, 1991). Although most fragile X males do not evidence hallucinations or delusions, some individuals may show distorted, tangential, and perseverative thinking and odd preoccupations (Hagerman, Levitas, & Rogers, 1992). The specific ways in which thought disorder differs across males with fragile X, autism, or PDD-NOS remain unclear. Given the lack of positive criteria for PDD in current nosology, it may be best for research to de-emphasize diagnostic issues and instead focus on the nature, course, and prevalence of thought disorder and other "PDD-like" behaviors in fragile X syndrome.

Asperger's Syndrome

In addition to PDD, Asperger's syndrome is another as yet unexplored way of capturing potential oddities in social relatedness, thought, and affect that are manifest by some higher functioning fragile X males. Individuals with Asperger's syndrome show adequate language skills and intelligence, yet are socially awkward and isolative; have difficulties with intimacy; are poor at reading social cues; and may show deviant nonverbal communication, bland affect, and limited, circumscribed interests (Wing, 1981). Consistent with the low frequency of fragile X men of average intelligence, only a handful of Asperger's cases have been reported (Gillberg, Steffenburg, & Jakobsson, 1987; Hagerman, 1989). Although infrequent, these cases are consistent with the spectrum of withdrawal, avoidance, and other problems in social relatedness shown by lower-functioning fragile X males, and as such, are in need of further study.

Females and Autism

The central role that socially avoidant behaviors assume in the phenomenology of fragile X syndrome gains further support from research on females with this disorder. Autism is uncommon in females in general, and presumably also in fragile X females. Although cases of autistic, fragile X females have been reported, most females are better described by recent studies that link their genetic status to social avoidance and anxiety. Having described autism and social avoidance in males, we now turn to a consideration of these features in females.

Of the 1,120 autistic subjects who were screened for fragile X syndrome listed in Table 7.1, approximately 90, or 8%, were females. None of these autistic females showed the fragile X marker upon testing. In the largest study to date, Cohen, Brown et al. (1989) screened 33 autistic females for the fragile X marker and found 4 fragile X cases. Collapsing across various prevalence figures, Cohen, Brown et al. (1989) estimate that 1.7% of fragile X females are autistic.

These relatively low rates are consistent with the 4 to 1 predominance of males to females with autism and with the limited number of clinical case descriptions of autistic, fragile X females. Three research groups (Bolton & Rutter, 1989; Gillberg, Ohlson, Wahlstrom, Steffenburg, & Blix, 1988; Hagerman, Chudley et al., 1986) have described a total of six moderately impaired, autistic, fragile X females. Cytogenetically, these females had high percentages of fragile cells, supporting relationships between symptom severity and high percentages of fragility.

Similar to males, research on the prevalence of autistic, fragile X females is susceptible to problems of ascertainment bias, sample size, and diagnostic inconsistencies. Although heightened professional awareness of possible autistic, fragile X females is desirable, the low estimated prevalence rate of these cases may actually exacerbate the methodological problems encountered in male prevalence studies. As such, research attention may be better focused on the majority of fragile X females, many of whom show emotional vulnerabilities that are both similar to and divergent from their male counterparts.

Females and Problems With Social Relatedness

Young girls with fragile X have been depicted as shy, socially avoidant, withdrawn, and anxious, with poor or fleeting eye contact (e.g., Hagerman, Jackson et al., 1992; Lachiewicz, 1992a). Shyness may be more pronounced in low IQ versus high IQ girls (Cronister et al., 1991), although socially withdrawn behavior has also been found in girls across the IQ spectrum (Lachiewicz, 1992a). Hagerman, Jackson et al. (1992) note that childhood shyness and social anxieties may become more problematic in adolescence due to age-related demands for sociability—features that may ultimately contribute to low self-esteem and depression.

In adulthood as well, many carrier females seem to be shy, anxious, and socially awkward, and some may become psychotic or depressed (Fryns, 1986; Reiss et al., 1986). In a pilot study of one family, Reiss et al. (1986) found three carrier women who suffered from either major affective or schizoaffective disorders. Although links between the fragile X marker and specific vulnerabilities to psychopathology were suggested, mothers of developmentally delayed children in general may also experience heightened depression and stress due to the demands of parenting a special needs child (e.g., Minnes, 1988).

To identify unique psychiatric features of average IQ, carrier females, Reiss, Hagerman, Vinogradov, Abrams, and King (1988) compared fragile X women with mothers of non-fragile X, developmentally delayed children. Using structured psychiatric interviews and scales, fragile X women were found to have poorer social and interpersonal skills, more unusual thoughts, and heightened emotional lability relative to control subjects. These features were consistent with higher rates of schizotypal personality disorder in the fragile X group, who also experienced an earlier onset of these problems than their counterparts.

Recent studies have confirmed features of shyness in carrier females, and related these observations to the genetic status of these women. Reiss, Freund, Vinogradov, Hagerman, and Cronister (1989) compared two groups of average IQ obligate carriers: those with maternal inheritance and positive fragility, and those with paternal inheritance or negative fragility. The maternal-inheritance group showed more schizophrenia-spectrum problems relative to the negative fragility group, including social withdrawal and difficulties in the organization and content of thoughts. Maternal-inheritance females also showed more social disability in adolescence, lower educational achievements, and more time away from work due to psychological problems.

These findings are clarified by Freund, Reiss, Hagerman, and Vinogradov (1992) and Sobesky (1992), who reported heightened schizotypal features among obligate carrier women with positive fragility relative to carriers with no evidence of the fragile site. These schizotypal features were characterized by language abnormalities and social withdrawal rather than by bizarre thinking or hallucinatory phenomena. Preliminary data suggest that some women with positive fragility tend to minimize or deny their problems; this finding needs further study (Sobesky, 1992).

Thus there is growing evidence that shyness, social withdrawal, or oddities in relating may characterize many carrier females with positive fragility. These features, coupled with socially avoidant behavior in males, suggest that both males and females with fragile X syndrome share disturbances in social relatedness. Cohen, Sudhalter et al. (1991) have speculated that fragile X syndrome may lead primarily to social avoidance, with autism as a severe, secondary, less common outcome. Social avoidance and shyness have not been observed consistently in other genetic, mental retardation disorders such as Prader-Willi syndrome or Down syndrome. Although these features suggest a unique fragile X phenotype, comparative studies are now needed that identify the extent to which shyness, social avoidance, and oddities in relating are shared with other genetic and nongenetic disorders.

ATTENTION DEFICITS
AND HYPERACTIVITY

In striking contrast to the fine-tuned research characteristic of the autism controversy, there has been little systematic research on attention deficits or hyperactivity in males or females with fragile X syndrome. This lack of detailed information is troubling because attention deficits and hyperactivity have long been documented informally in the literature, and these difficulties are encountered much more frequently in fragile X syndrome than autistic disorder per se.

Inattention and Hyperactivity in Males

Attentional and hyperactivity problems are consistently found in many males with fragile X syndrome. Fryns et al. (1984) observed that hyperactivity and concentration difficulties were the most striking behavioral problems encountered in their sample of 21 males. Largo and Schinzel (1985) and Fryns et al. (1984) report that these features were present to varying degrees in all of their respective subjects. Lower percentages of these behaviors were reported by Rhoads (1984) and Simko et al. (1989): 41% and 65%, respectively. As none of these studies reported how attention deficits or hyperactivity were measured, the variability in rates— from 41% to 100%—may stem from differences in behavioral judgments across researchers.

Using more rigorous assessment procedures, Bregman et al. (1988) found that all but one of their sample of 14 males (93%) met DSM-III (APA, 1980) criteria for attention deficit hyperactivity disorder, or ADHD. Also using systematic assessment procedures, Hagerman (1987) found that 73% of 37 prepubertal fragile X males exhibited elevated scores on the Connors rating scale, a widely used questionnaire of attention deficits and hyperactivity.

Attention deficits and hyperactivity do not appear to be correlated with IQ; in other words, these difficulties are manifest in boys across the IQ spectrum (e.g., Borghgraef et al., 1987; Fryns et al., 1984). As such, a relatively high IQ does not serve as a protective factor against these significant behavioral problems, which are often the primary presenting issues that bring undiagnosed, higher-functioning boys to the clinical setting (Hagerman, Kemper, & Hudson, 1985).

In contrast to IQ, preliminary findings suggest that there is a significant relationship between attentional problems and age. Largo and Schinzel (1985) report that hyperactivity may emerge by the second year, and others have noted that these behaviors are most frequent and intense in preschool and school-age boys (Borghgraef et al., 1987; Fryns et al., 1984). These problems may decline with age—hyperactivity seems to diminish over time in many males—but attention and concentration problems persist into adulthood (Dykens et al., 1988; Rhoads, 1984).

The high rates of attention and activity problems reported in most studies may be associated with the use of referred or clinic samples; in contrast, nonreferred fragile X males may be less prone to exhibit these difficulties. Although the prevalence of ADHD among nonreferred fragile X males remains unknown, these features may be present in 15% of mentally retarded persons of mixed etiologies (Jacobson, 1982). The specificity of ADHD in fragile X can be tested by comparing ADHD symptoms in fragile X and matched control subjects from both clinic and nonreferred samples. To date, there have been three such comparative studies, one of which controlled for referral bias.

Borghgraef et al. (1987) found that fragile X boys aged 2 to 12 exhibited approximately twice as much attention deficit disorder as matched controls, although this difference was not statistically significant. Low frustration tolerance was particularly prevalent in fragile X boys. Controlling for ascertainment bias, Einfeld, Hall, and Levy (1991) compared 45 fragile X males, aged 2 through adulthood, to matched controls. The groups did not differ in impulsivity, inattention, hyperactivity, or aggressive behavior. Similarly, comparing institutionalized fragile X adults with nonspecific and autistic males, Dykens et al. (1988) found no group differences in hyperactivity, poor concentration, and impulsivity.

It may be that the lack of group differences in the Einfeld et al. (1991) and Dykens et al. (1988) studies is associated with age. Einfeld et al.'s fragile X subjects had a mean age of 12.6 years, and Dykens et al.'s subjects averaged 37.8 years of age. It may be, however, that hyperactivity, and to a lesser extent inattention, diminish with age: Borghgraef et al. (1987) reported that 80% of fragile X preschoolers exhibited attention deficit disorder, whereas only 50% of older children aged 7 to 12 did so. Between-group differences in hyperactivity, aggression, and inattention are thus more likely to be evident in young children. The extent to which inattention and hyperactivity are shared with other retarded samples or are unique to fragile X syndrome thus remains unclear; further studies are needed that compare young versus old fragile X males with suitably matched comparison groups.

Inattention and Hyperactivity in Females

Inattention and hyperactivity have been observed recently in girls with fragile X syndrome. Borghgraef et al. (1990) reported mild to moderate attention deficit disorder in all seven of their female subjects aged 6 to 13, with more pronounced hyperactivity in the two youngest girls. Using Achenbach's Child Behavior Checklist, Lachiewicz (1992a) found elevated hyperactive-scale scores in 47% of her sample of 38 girls aged 4 to 11. Although IQ did not correlate with hyperactive scores, there was a tendency for higher IQ girls to have more hyperactivity and other behavior problems than their lower-functioning counterparts. Hagerman, Jackson et al. (1992) compared ADHD symptoms in 32 fragile X girls aged 1 to 18 with their 19 fragile X negative sisters. Fragile X girls exhibited significantly higher mean scores on the Connors rating scale than unaffected sisters. Ten fragile X girls met DSM-III-R criteria for ADHD, whereas none of the fragile X negative sisters did so. These researchers noted that fragile X, ADHD girls exhibited more problems with inattention, impulsivity, and distractibility as opposed to hyperactivity. Similar to trends of ADHD in boys versus girls in the general population, ADHD seems less prevalent and intense in fragile X girls than boys. Studies are needed with both fragile X boys and girls that identify the developmental course of ADHD symptoms and that document differences in ADHD symptoms in referred and nonreferred fragile X cases. Research that compares ADHD symptoms across fragile X and other developmentally delayed groups is also necessary. Further, studies have not yet described how ADHD might be associated with other impulse control problems often seen in fragile X syndrome, such as aggression and temper tantrums, or how ADHD impacts upon learning. It would be particularly helpful, for example, to compare males with and without ADHD (or with different severity levels of ADHD) on sequential processing and short-term memory tasks.

OTHER DISORDERS
IN FRAGILE X SYNDROME

Other psychiatric, physical, and genetic problems associated with fragile X syndrome include depression, Tourette's syndrome, seizure disorders, sleep apnea, and Klinefelter's syndrome. Although these other disorders are less common in fragile X syndrome than ADHD, social anxiety, and relatedness problems, and usually autism as well, each involves symptoms that may detract from optimal functioning.

Depression

In Males. Compared with disturbances in social relatedness and attention, depressive features have been observed less consistently in fragile

X males. Depression may be less frequently reported due to assessment problems; primarily, differentiating affective symptoms from behavior problems that are commonly found in mentally retarded persons (Sovner, 1989). Limited verbal skills and cognitive delay may make it difficult for many fragile X males to label and report accurately internal states such as sadness, hopelessness, self-deprecation, or guilt. As such, Sovner (1989) and Tranebjaerg and Orum (1991) suggest that the best indicators of depression in fragile X and other mentally retarded groups are a worsening of maladaptive behavior, loss of skills, and neurovegetative signs (e.g., fatigue, changes in sleep and appetite).

Given these measurement problems, the prevalence of depression or other affective disorders in the fragile X population remains unknown. To date, only a few fragile X males with affective disorder have been reported, with diagnoses of either major depression or manic-depressive illness (Mendlewicz & Hirsch, 1991; Sovner, 1989; Tranebjaerg & Orum, 1991). These males typically exhibited marked increases in various maladaptive behaviors, decreases in adaptive functioning, and, in some cases, excessive worries and guilt. These cases have led to speculation of a possible linkage between a locus for affective illness and the fragile X site (Mendlewicz & Hirsh, 1991).

Consistent with mentally retarded persons in general, it may be that persons with fragile X syndrome have certain life experiences or personality features that serve as precursors to depressive symptoms. These features include multiple failure experiences, low expectations for success, turning to others for solutions to problems, diminished pleasure with certain tasks, and a low ideal self-image (Zigler & Hodapp, 1986b). Although many of these experiences seem ripe for setting the stage for depression, none of them have yet been studied in fragile X syndrome, including how they might be exacerbated by the predisposition toward social avoidance found in this syndrome.

The possibility of depressive features in affected males should not be overlooked. Although depression may not be as prominent a feature in fragile X males as social relatedness or activity problems, this may be simply because the manifestations of depression are not well understood. Further research is needed that examines a range of possible expressions of depression in these males, including symptoms that are less dependent upon verbal and cognitive abilities.

In Females. Relative to affected males, research on depression in carrier females is facilitated by the higher-functioning levels of these women, and perhaps by the greater proportion of depressive symptomatology among females in general. Reiss et al. (1988) found elevated rates of intermittent, recurring depressive episodes in carrier females relative to a control group of mothers of developmentally delayed children. These episodes tended to be of mild to moderate severity, and were also characterized by feelings of guilt and self-reproach.

Comparisons between carrier females with positive versus negative fragility have generally resulted in comparable rates of chronic affective disorder and dysthymia (or enduring feelings of sadness) (Freund et al., 1992; Reiss et al, 1989; Sobesky, 1992). Similar rates of depression between positive versus negative fragility groups may be associated with the stress and demands of parenting developmentally delayed children with fragile X syndrome (Freund et al., 1992; Reiss et al., 1989). Lingering self-blame or guilt for transmitting a genetic disorder to their children may also be present in these two groups of women.

There is some suggestion that carriers with positive fragility may be more vulnerable to episodes of major depression (heightened feelings of sadness, hopelessness, and guilt, and neurovegetative signs) than cytogenetically negative females (Sobesky, 1992). However, this difference has not been observed consistently (Freund et al., 1992; Reiss et al., 1989), and further studies are needed that compare dysthymia with major depression in positive versus negative fragility women.

Tourette's Syndrome

Tourette's syndrome is a childhood onset disorder characterized by vocal and motor tics that wax and wane throughout development. Only a few cases of Tourette's syndrome in fragile X patients have been reported (Bregman et al. 1988; Hagerman, 1987; Kerbeshian, Burd, & Martsolf, 1984), including one boy with complex motor and vocal tics that included throat clearing, barking, and coprolalia, or repetitive swearing.

Similar to fragile X syndrome, Tourette's syndrome is often associated with hyperactivity; but unlike fragile X, individuals with Tourette's syndrome generally have average intelligence (Dykens, Leckman et al., 1991). It may be that Tourette's syndrome is occasionally found in fragile X individuals, as it has been in Down syndrome and in mentally retarded persons of mixed etiologies. Many fragile X males exhibit motor stereotypes (e.g., hand rubbing, flapping, and biting) and odd, perseverative verbalizations that are consistent with diagnoses of pervasive developmental disorders (PDD) or autism. As such, it may be difficult to distinguish between the vocal and motor tics characteristic of Tourette's syndrome and the stereotypes often found in fragile X males, some of whom may have PDD or autism.

Seizure Disorders

Unlike the many behavioral problems encountered in fragile X individuals, seizures have not been widely recognized or discussed. As such, Hecht (1991) and others have called for increased awareness among professionals and parents of this often neglected problem.

The majority of individuals with fragile X syndrome do not have seizures. Based on pooled prevalence estimates, the rate of seizures in fragile X males ranges from 19% (Hecht, 1991) to 25% (Wisniewski, Segan, Miezejeski, Sersen, & Rudelli, 1991).

Seizures in fragile X syndrome tend to have a childhood or early adolescent onset, are typically infrequent, and seem to spontaneously remit by young adulthood (Wisniewski et al., 1991). This pattern has also been described by Musumeci et al. (1991), who identified an association between fragile X syndrome and benign childhood epilepsy. This association, and its underlying EEG pattern, may be specific to fragile X syndrome relative to other individuals with developmental delay (Musumeci et al., 1988). Although there is thus evidence that most seizures in fragile X are benign and remit with age, some fragile X individuals continue to manifest seizures in their adult years (Musumeci et al., 1991). These seizures are generally well-controlled with standard anticonvulsant medication.

As is the case with seizures in many types of mental retardation, the cause of seizures in fragile X syndrome remains unknown. Some researchers have speculated that seizures are not necessarily a result of fragile X syndrome, but are instead idiopathic in origin, or the result of a genetic loading for epilepsy that is independent of fragile X (Vieregge & Froster-Iskenius, 1989). Others, however, have implicated commonalities in genetic deficits associated with fragile X syndrome and benign forms of childhood epilepsy (Musumeci et al., 1988). Research is needed that clarifies this issue and that explores relationships among EEG anomalies, genetic status, and behavior.

Sleep Apnea

Recent work by Tirosh and Borochowitz (1992) suggests that fragile X males may be at increased risk for sleep apnea. Four out of seven males who underwent sleep studies were found to exhibit severe to mild apnea. These findings may be related to the narrow facial structure and oropharyngeal (nose and throat) cavity in fragile X syndrome, and to hypotonic oropharyngeal muscles that were found in these males during REM sleep. The type of apnea associated with sudden infant death syndrome, prolonged expiratory apnea, was found in two fragile X subjects in Tirosh and Borochowitz's (1992) study. As such, prolonged expiratory apnea may be associated with the increased occurrence of sudden infant death syndrome found in fragile X infants (Fryns, Moerman, Gilis, d'Espallier, & Van den Berghe, 1988). As sleep apnea apparently contributes to behavioral and developmental problems in normal children, Tirosh and Borochowitz (1992) urge physicians to be alerted to the possibility that obstructive sleep apnea may exacerbate behavioral problems commonly found in fragile X syndrome. It remains unknown, however, how widespread this problem is in the fragile X population, and prevalence studies are needed to clarify these preliminary findings.

Klinefelter's Syndrome

Klinefelter's syndrome is a genetic disorder found in males who have an extra X chromosome (XXY): tall stature; small, soft testes; and average intelligence—although in a minority of cases, mild mental retardation is present. There have been at least a dozen case reports of males with co-occurring Klinefelter and fragile X syndromes (e.g., Pecile & Filippi, 1991). When these disorders co-occur, men generally show a more severe clinical presentation than when each disorder occurs alone. It may be that there is an increased association between these two genetic disorders as a result of the fragile X mutation predisposing the X chromosome to nondisjunction (Watson et al., 1988). Further research is necessary that documents the behavioral, physical, and genetic features of these unusual cases.

SUMMARY

The complexity of maladaptive behaviors exhibited by males and females with fragile X syndrome underscores the importance of identifying psychopathology within specific etiological groups. Although many males with fragile X syndrome exhibit a variety of autistic behaviors, it is doubtful whether the prevalence of autistic disorder in these males is greater than expected given their levels of mental retardation. Social anxieties, avoidance, shyness, and gaze aversion seem to characterize many males with fragile X syndrome. Although these features, coupled with certain autistic-like behaviors and thought disorder, may be captured by diagnoses such as PDD or Asperger's syndrome, considerable light was shed on the autism controversy when studies moved away from diagnostic labels and instead focused on fine-tuned analyses of fragile X behavior.

In contrast to studies on autism and the spectrum of socially avoidant behavior, there has been little research on the attention deficits and hyperactivity that characterize so many males, especially younger boys, across the IQ spectrum. The relationship between these ADHD symptoms and learning, sequential processing, impulse control problems, likelihood of referral to a clinical setting, and adult outcome remains unknown.

Similar to males, many carrier females have difficulties with social relatedness and may be shy, withdrawn, socially avoidant, and anxious, and they may show poor eye contact. Attention deficits, usually with less hyperactivity, are also seen in fragile X girls. Some carrier females have increased vulnerabilities toward depressive episodes and disorganized thinking; these features need to be clarified with respect to DNA status.

Further specification of the fragile X phenotype requires more fine-tuned behavioral analyses that describe attention deficits, hyperactivity, social avoidance, anxiety, repetitive and stereotypical behaviors, thought disorder, depressive symptomatology, and personality functioning in both affected males and carrier females. Each of these problems needs to be examined in relation to age, sex, IQ, and DNA status.

In addition to behavioral studies within fragile X syndrome, comparisons also should be made *between* fragile X subjects and persons with other genetic disorders (e.g., Down syndrome, Prader-Willi syndrome) and with other types of developmental delay (e.g., autism, PDD, learning disabilities). These between-group comparisons can identify the extent to which behavioral problems are unique or shared, ultimately providing a clearer description of the fragile X phenotype and leading to more refined treatment approaches.

8

INTERVENTION AND TREATMENT

Although various forms of gene therapy may be possible in the future, presently there is no cure for fragile X syndrome. We also lack standard interventions that have proven consistently helpful across all fragile X individuals. There are, however, many available intervention strategies that have optimized functioning in affected males and carrier females and provided support for their families. These interventions have included parent and family support services and groups; a host of recommendations for special educational programming and occupational, speech/language, and behavior therapies; and less frequently, psychotherapy and pharmacology (i.e., medication).

Although this chapter discusses each of these interventions separately for heuristic purposes, optimal interventions are typically integrative in nature. Fragile X students may, for example, do better when behavior modification techniques used in the classroom are also integrated into other settings, such as in occupational therapy or at home. Similarly, medications work best when they are coupled with appropriate supportive services, such as a suitable special education program or ongoing psychotherapy. Thus despite the organization of this chapter into discrete types of intervention, many of these efforts are likely to work best as an integrated whole.

These different intervention strategies also need to be integrated in ways that prove uniquely optimal for each person and that are sensitive to each person's development and changing needs. As such, specific treatments will differ both within and across affected males and carrier females and their families. Given the need for multiple, developmentally sensitive, and well-integrated services, it is often helpful for a health or mental health professional to follow the fragile X child and family on a long-term basis to help organize and maintain continuity of care.

FAMILY SUPPORT

Immediate and extended family members may show a variety of emotional reactions to the news that their family is affected with fragile X syndrome. Many parents—especially parents of older males—may experience relief in finally receiving an explanation of their child's developmental delays. It is also common, however, for parents to blame themselves and to feel guilty—as Patricia did in the case story. In addition to blaming themselves, family members also may be angry and upset with one another, or with professionals involved in their child's care, and be unsure about the best way to tell other family members about the syndrome's associated risks. The diagnosis of fragile X syndrome also has been observed to strengthen familial support and facilitate communication in a positive, growthful manner.

Many of these emotional reactions are associated with processes that parents and families often go through in coming to terms with the loss of an idealized, "perfect" child. It is commonly assumed that parents of handicapped children pass through three stages of mourning the loss of their nonimpaired infant: a generalized shock reaction, including denial; emotional disorganization, such as anger or depression; and then emotional organization and acceptance, which pave the way for a realistic plan of care for the child (Solnit & Stark, 1961).

More recent work, however, supports the idea that parents of handicapped children may "revisit" sorrow and mourning when they are confronted with reminders of their child's developmental delay; for example, when a younger peer surpasses the child, or when the child first enters school or becomes an adolescent (Wikler, Wasow, & Hatfield, 1981). Further, the timing and intensity of this recurrent mourning may differ across various handicapping conditions (Hodapp, Dykens, Evans, & Merighi, 1992). Therapy and counseling thus might help to prepare parents for periodic and unexpected resurgences of grief and sorrow.

Applying concepts of mourning and adjustment to fragile X syndrome, Meryash (1989) suggested that mothers of fragile X children learn to cope with their child's special needs, and that their perceptions of burden in raising a handicapped child may lessen over time. Although these findings may reflect the tendency for women with positive fragility to minimize or deny their problems (Sobesky, 1992), they are consistent with the idea that perceptions of burden and stress vary across etiological groups. Mothers of children with Down syndrome, for example, experience less stress and a more positive outlook than mothers of autistic and neurologically impaired children (Goldberg, Marcovitch, MacGregor, & Lojkasek, 1986; Holroyd & MacArthur, 1978).

Perceptions of burden and the stressors of parenting a developmentally delayed child thus differ over time and from one etiological group to another. Interventions aimed at providing support to the parents and families of fragile X children should be adjusted accordingly (Dykens & Leckman, 1990). For many families with a fragile X member, intervention may consist of family or individual therapy in times of heightened stress or of enrolling in a parent support group. Many communities now have fragile X support groups; these groups are particularly helpful in alleviating feelings of isolation, gaining emotional support, and sharing effective behavioral management techniques. For communities without a fragile X group, the National Fragile X Syndrome Association[1] offers suggestions for starting groups.

Other families, however, do not voluntarily enroll in therapeutic services or seek out a parent support group. This may be particularly true for carrier females who are shy and avoidant and who deny or minimize their problems. These women may be hard to engage in services, posing a challenge to interventionists. This challenge becomes even more daunting when multiple children in the family are affected with fragile X syndrome, and in families with mothers who are delayed or less educated and who may not cope well with parenting a special needs child (Meryash, 1989). These families are at increased risk for distress and disorganization and may require intensive or long-term intervention (Dykens & Leckman, 1990).

One way of supporting these at-risk families is through parent aid and at-home intervention programs. Although the specifics of these programs vary, they typically include a parent aid who models limit-setting and other parenting skills in the home, provides caregivers with emotional support and encouragement, and guides the family through educational and social service agencies. At-home intervention models also increase the likelihood that families will remain involved in supportive services or seek them out at a later time.

The role of fathers in both at-risk and better organized families remains unclear. In some families, the special demands of the fragile X child may strengthen the marital relationship and pull family members together in a positive and growthful manner. In other families, the mother's psychiatric or cognitive vulnerabilities may result in heightened dependencies upon her husband, who may, in turn, become overburdened and distressed. Research and clinical interest in fathers in fragile X families has paled in comparison with carrier females, and research is needed that documents the assets and special needs of these men.

EDUCATIONAL INTERVENTIONS

The most salient social service available to children with fragile X syndrome is the school. Yet to a large extent, a child's etiology of mental retardation has never played a major role in special education efforts. Instead, children are much more likely to be grouped according to their overall level of impairment, or integrated into regular classrooms with little regard for etiology-specific behaviors. Hodapp and Dykens (1991, 1992) emphasize the need for etiology-based educational approaches in a variety of genetic disorders, many of which could be implemented in mainstreamed or special education classes.

Many parental concerns about their children are heightened when they begin the process of securing appropriate educational services. Frustrations may arise when well-meaning parents try to get the "best" educational services possible for their child and are confronted with negotiating potentially unfamiliar educational systems and state agencies. Both parents and educational professionals need to be sensitive to these potential frustrations and aim to maintain supportive, nonadversarial roles with one another.

Recommendations regarding both how and when to intervene with fragile X students may be derived from their profiles and trajectories of cognitive development (see Chapter 4), and from their predispositions to certain maladaptive behaviors (see Chapter 7). Ultimately, however, any particular student's educational programming should be based on the student's individual testing and patterns of strength and weakness.

How Best to Intervene Educationally. Many fragile X students do not respond well to problems that demand sequential processing, or breaking tasks down into their component parts and placing them in serial or temporal order (e.g., left to right, first to last). Rather, they respond best to interventions that emphasize simultaneous processing, or an approach in which the overall meaning of the task is conveyed with visual-spatial stimuli. This gestalt-like learning also might include placing stimuli in a context that has a particular meaning for each student. Many fragile X students thus learn in a seemingly incidental manner by forming associations among stimuli in a context that has relevance for them, or that uses visual-spatial processing.

Fragile X students generally do well with pictures, models and diagrams, and computer games or tasks that have a visual-perceptual orientation. Students also may do well with visual approaches to reading and math as provided by rebus symbols (Hinton, 1991) and the Logo reading and math programs (Braden, 1989; Braden & Woods, 1992). These reading approaches match words with symbols or with commonly encountered logos in the child's environment (e.g., stores, road signs, gas stations, restaurants), then gradually fade the visual cue. Mathematical games or worksheets that exploit each students' particular interests (even their perseverative topics) also have been shown to be captivating for fragile X students. In addition to their perseverative topics, these reading approaches and math games may also take advantage of the strengths in vocabulary shown by many fragile X students.

Hands-on activities, such as cooking and role-playing real-life situations (e.g., going to the grocery store or gas station), also serve as high-interest ways of teaching both academic and adaptive skills. Lessons taught in these types of activities include measuring and counting, taking turns, waiting in line, following social expectations, recognizing labels, money concepts, and so forth. Many special educators have found these approaches quite helpful, and they are derived from well-established cognitive profiles of the disorder. Still, the efficacy of these educational strategies with fragile X students has not yet been systematically examined, especially relative to more traditional, sequentially based teaching strategies.

The short attention span, anxiety, repetitive behavior, aggression, and self-abuse shown by many fragile X students may be particularly heightened by excessive environmental stimuli, uncertainty in the school day, a change in classroom routine, and transitions. To avoid being overwhelmed by these events, many fragile X students do well in classrooms that minimize visual and auditory distractors, and that maintain a consistent and predictable routine. Visual cues, such as snapshots, diagrams, or calendars of the school day, and anticipated departures from the normal routine may help the fragile X student remain calm. Other calming techniques that have proven helpful include deep breathing, humming, singing, listening to music, time out in a bean bag chair or a nest of pillows, and deep pressure and other forms of touch (Scharfenaker, Hickman, & Braden, 1991).

Occupational therapy that includes a variety of sensory integration techniques is often recommended for young students to address poor muscle tone, tactile defensiveness, and fine and gross motor problems. Most boys also benefit from speech and language services that target weaknesses in pragmatics, grammar, and speech. As math seems to be an area of consistent weakness in fragile X syndrome, extra help is often needed in this subject as well. Some fragile X boys may be "pulled out" of regular education classrooms for specialized math services and occupational and speech/language therapies. Other fragile X students may be enrolled in self-contained, special education classrooms. Regardless of placement, educational programming should strive to integrate the multiple services needed by the fragile X student in ways that optimize predictability and that minimize distractibility and sensory overload.

The Timing of Intervention and Adult Services. Research suggests that it may be best to intervene with fragile X males at younger ages. This recommendation stems from the developmental plateaus encountered in some fragile X males around early to mid-adolescence. "The earlier the better" may be the best strategy of capitalizing on each student's learning potential, prior to possible shifts or plateaus in development. Although early intervention is advocated for many at-risk children, it seems particularly critical with fragile X males given the later plateauing that may be specific to this syndrome.

Interventionists should, however, continue to emphasize the acquisition of adaptive and vocational skills in older adolescent and adult fragile X males. This recommendation is underscored by the critical role that adaptive behavior plays in the long-term success of mentally retarded persons in general. Similarly, involvement in vocational training programs serves to optimize independence and adaptive functioning. Although there are no available data on the vocational needs of older fragile X males, many of the techniques offered for the classroom setting have direct relevance for the work environment. Jobs that emphasize visual skills and strengths in adaptive daily living skills—which may be quite pronounced in older males—are recommended, as are work settings that minimize distractibility and sensory overload. Fragile X adults may, for example, work best in small settings that have few people and predictable tasks; large, congested settings, such as fast-food restaurants or grocery stores, may be more difficult for the fragile X adult.

Future studies need to document whether these recommendations for the "how and when" of educational-vocational interventions are successful relative to other teaching strategies. In addition, it remains unclear to what extent these recommendations are applicable to other special education students, or are unique to fragile X syndrome. Research is also needed that identifies the vocational needs of adult fragile X males, including how these needs shift with the aging process.

BEHAVIORAL TECHNIQUES

Many persons with fragile X syndrome may respond well to behavior modification techniques that have long been used to treat a variety of behavioral problems in mentally retarded individuals in general (see Cipani [1989] for a review). These techniques can both teach desirable behaviors and extinguish maladaptive behaviors. Although often used in educational, vocational, and institutional settings, these techniques also can be adapted for parental use in the home.

Positive and negative reinforcements are used to increase desirable behaviors, and punishment is used to reduce undesirable behaviors. Positive reinforcement (e.g., social approval—a smile, "nice job," or "good boy"; stickers; food; opportunity to play a favorite game; etc.) and punishment (ranging from reprimands and time outs to mild electric shock) are more frequently used than negative reinforcement (escaping from an aversive experience). Various combinations of punishment and positive reinforcement have been used to treat a variety of behavioral problems in persons with mental retardation, including aggression, hyperactivity, noncompliance, self-injury, and stereotypies (e.g., Matson & Gorman-Smith, 1986).

Many fragile X males exhibit maladaptive behaviors such as aggression, self-abuse (e.g., hand biting), gaze avoidance, and repetitive behaviors (e.g., hand flapping, perseverative speech, spinning) that have proven quite amenable to behavioral interventions in mentally retarded persons of mixed etiologies. These interventions include time out, positive reinforcement, and shaping behaviors; higher-functioning males may also respond to a token economy program or self-monitoring techniques.

To date, however, studies have not yet documented the efficacy of these techniques in either high- or low-functioning fragile X males. Indeed, very little is known about the differential effectiveness of behavioral techniques in persons with various etiologies. For example, unlike persons with Down syndrome or Prader-Willi syndrome, fragile X males may show deficits in sequential processing or a proneness to anxiety or perseverative thinking that require special consideration in behavioral programming for them. It may be optimal to supplement traditional behavioral approaches with fragile X males with various calming techniques or with an emphasis on visual stimuli and cues as opposed to verbal input.

PSYCHOTHERAPEUTIC INTERVENTIONS

Some mildly affected males and carrier females may benefit from involvement in psychotherapy and counseling. The therapeutic needs of these two groups, however, are quite different, and the success of psychotherapy with either sex has yet to be compared with the success of other intervention models.

Therapy With Males. Mentally retarded individuals in general are at increased risk for failure experiences; social rejection, stigma, and infantilization from others; and heightened dependencies upon others. These features may be associated with heightened conflicts or distress that are amenable to a variety of therapeutic approaches.

As summarized by Bregman (1991), psychotherapy with mildly retarded persons features unique goals and strategies. Therapeutic goals may include: learning adaptive ways of coping with feelings of anger or resentment related to social stigma; realizing one's cognitive limitations; increasing self-esteem, independence, and emancipation from caregivers; and learning new social skills.

Many fragile X males have difficulties with attention and auditory processing, and these individuals may require considerable refocusing and repetition in therapy. Sessions may also need to be frequent, short, structured, and oriented toward a single goal. Other therapeutic tactics include a focus on current as opposed to past issues; the use of language, concepts, and activities that match the client's mental age; and a willingness for the therapist to engage in a range of activities such as role-playing, modeling, drawing, playing, redirecting, calming, and so forth (Bregman, 1991; Hurley, 1989).

Therapy With Females. Females with fragile X syndrome have a unique set of therapeutic needs that can be accommodated in a variety of ways. The shyness and social anxieties exhibited by some young fragile X girls could be addressed in therapy groups aimed at social-skills training and play skills with peers, or involvements in structured after-school activities that foster successful experiences for participants.

Adult carrier females may have a host of psychological concerns, many of which can be addressed in family interventions and parent support groups. For some women, however, individual therapy may also be helpful to address shyness and social anxiety, depression, coping with specific learning problems or disabilities, low self-esteem and guilt associated with having a transmittable genetic disorder, grief and sorrow in having a handicapped child, difficulties in coping with the demands of a developmentally delayed child or children, and worries regarding the reproductive decisions faced by their carrier daughters.

Hagerman and Sobesky (1989) suggest that many carrier women may benefit from individual therapy that first decreases social anxiety and then uses relaxation and biofeedback techniques to increase feelings of efficacy and control. Therapy might also include building social skills with various cognitive self-monitoring techniques, grief work aimed at resolving the loss of an ideal self (i.e., a self with no genetic vulnerability), and adopting a more realistic self-concept.

PHARMACOLOGY

As described in Chapter 7, many fragile X males and, to a lesser extent, carrier females exhibit attention deficits and hyperactivity. These problems may be particularly apparent in the preschool and school-age years, and they also affect persons throughout the full range of intellectual functioning. Although the environmental and educational interventions previously described often alleviate these attentional and activity problems, medications in conjunction with environmental manipulations may also prove helpful in reducing these behaviors.

Stimulant Medication. Recent data suggest that stimulant medications may help target hyperactivity and inattention in many fragile X males and females. Hagerman, Murphy, and Wittenberger (1988) conducted a double-blind crossover study assessing methylphenidate versus dextroamphetamine in 15 fragile X children. Using multiple pre- and post-measures of attention and hyperactivity, they found that 10 of their 15 subjects showed a positive response to medication. Methylphenidate offered more consistent improvements, whereas dextroamphetamine created more side effects in some boys, primarily heightened irritability and lability. Hagerman et al. (1988) and others thus recommend trials of stimulant medication in hyperactive and inattentive fragile X boys and girls. Although other medications, such as tricyclics, have been used to treat attention deficits and hyperactivity in children in general, they have not yet been systematically evaluated in double-blind studies with fragile X children. Leckman (1987) reported positive responses to clonidine in open medication trials with several hyperactive fragile X boys; the effectiveness of clonidine also awaits further study.

The Folic Acid Controversy. Recall that Sutherland (1977) found that cytogenetic observation of the fragile X marker required use of a folate-deficient culture medium. In light of this finding, it was hypothesized that giving folic acid, one of the B vitamins, to affected individuals might produce beneficial effects (Harpey, 1982; Lejune, 1982). The effectiveness of folic acid on hyperactivity, autistic-like behavior, and learning was subsequently examined in more than a dozen open medication trials and carefully controlled double-blinded studies. Results from these studies are mixed. Most fragile X subjects showed no behavioral gains associated with folic acid, while subtle improvements in hyperactivity and inattention were occasionally reported only in young, prepubescent boys and girls.

Interestingly, this flurry of research on folic acid in fragile X syndrome occurred in the same time period as studies assessing vitamin treatment in persons with Down syndrome and with nonspecific mental retardation. Despite initial claims that vitamins resulted in behavioral and intellectual improvements in these groups, carefully controlled studies failed to replicate any of these findings. In the larger mental retardation field, then, vitamin therapy was once viewed as a promising intervention, and now joins a rather lengthy list of failed "miracle cures" (see Zigler & Hodapp [1986c] for a review). The initial excitement regarding folic acid's potential in fragile X syndrome has also subsided, and there is no evidence from recent genetic findings that support its continued use. Still, folic acid remains controversial. Some are encouraged by its effects (e.g., Hagerman, Jackson et al., 1992; Ho, Glahn, & Ho, 1988; Simensen & Rogers, 1989) and assert that no harmful effects of folic acid have yet been reported. Others, however, are skeptical of the routine use of folic acid and claim that its usefulness remains unproven (e.g., Brown et al., 1984; Rosenblatt et al., 1985). Some have admonished that folic acid may indeed be harmful in that it offers false hope to parents—perhaps of a "miracle cure"—potentially leading to discouragement and rejection of other, more well-established environmental interventions or medical treatments.

Other Medications

In Males. Psychotropic medications in mentally retarded persons work best when they are administered to individuals who suffer from a known psychiatric disorder. Often, however, medications are used to treat isolated symptoms instead of a specific psychiatric syndrome. Neuroleptics are often used in this manner and have been widely used to treat a variety of behavioral problems in mentally retarded individuals.

Many fragile X males exhibit problems with impulsive and aggressive outbursts; repetitive, stereotypical behaviors; and odd preoccupations. Consistent with mentally retarded persons in general, a variety of psychotropic medications has been given to fragile X individuals to target these behavioral problems. These medications have been administered in open clinical trials, and to date, there are no systematic studies that speak to their specific usefulness in fragile X syndrome. Some medications may be more or less effective within certain subgroups of fragile X individuals; for example, those with and without autistic disorder or ADHD. Considerable research thus is needed to establish the effectiveness of psychotropic medications in fragile X individuals of varying ages and IQs, and who exhibit a variety of behavioral problems.

In Females. Some affected fragile X females have been described as anxious, isolative, and depressed, and showing oddities in thinking. Although there are a variety of psychotropic medications that are used to treat anxiety, depression, and thought disorganization, none have yet been systematically assessed in fragile X females.

In a preliminary report, Sobesky (1992) found that fragile X women were more apt to have taken psychotropic medication at least once in their lives compared to non-fragile X mothers of developmentally delayed children. Fragile X women were less likely to engage in counseling than control mothers, and they also were more apt to use medication than counseling services. These findings speak to the challenge of engaging some fragile X females in services, and they also emphasize the importance of flexible treatment approaches that include various familial support and at-home intervention strategies.

SUMMARY

Although there is presently no cure for fragile X syndrome, the multiple interventions described in this chapter have proven helpful to affected fragile X individuals, as well as to their families, teachers, therapists, and other service providers. Interventions need to be well-integrated, consistent across multiple settings, and sensitive to the development and changing needs of the individual. The familial, educational, behavioral, therapeutic, and pharmacologic recommendations described in this chapter stemmed directly from fragile X profiles and trajectories of cognitive, adaptive, and linguistic functioning summarized throughout the book, as well as from maladaptive and psychiatric features discussed in Chapter 7. Although these recommendations are thus well-grounded, studies are now needed that formally establish their effectiveness relative to other kinds of interventions and to other developmentally delayed groups.

NOTE

1. For more information on parent support groups, contact the National Fragile X Foundation, 1441 York Street, Suite 215, Denver, CO 80206; 1-800-668-8765.

EPILOGUE

Fragile X syndrome presents a host of unresolved challenges to families, schools, research practices, and society at large that need to be addressed in the years ahead. For families, fragile X syndrome is unique relative to other developmental disorders in that multiple family members may be affected, including mothers, siblings, and distant relatives. Families must also cope with informing others in the family about the syndrome's associated risks. These features may heighten familial stress and pose a particular challenge to service providers (see Chapter 8).

Technological advances in identifying fragile X syndrome and in prenatal testing also pose novel decisions for many couples. What, for example, will couples decide if they face having an unaffected child with a pre-mutation, yet knowing that their grandchildren would likely be fully affected with fragile X syndrome? These unique dilemmas, as well as family planning choices among carrier females and nonpenetrant males, need immediate attention, especially if large-scale screening programs are implemented.

Educationally, fragile X students often present with specific behavioral problems and styles of learning that need to be acknowledged in individualized educational programs. Yet many educators de-emphasize etiology and instead favor generic or noncategorical services for their developmentally delayed students (Rowitz, 1988). Special educators thus need to find ways of working with fragile X profiles and behaviors despite the tendency to minimize the importance of etiology.

Within research on mental retardation, fragile X syndrome has already imposed a modification of the well-established two-group approach. Many other disorders are presumed to have a genetic cause, but at present can only be identified by clinical data (e.g., Finucane, Kurtz, & Scott, 1992). Given recent technological advances, many of these unspecified mental retardation disorders are likely to be specified in the years ahead.

These advances will further modify the two-group approach, and they also may result in innovative gene therapies and new means of preventing genetic causes of mental retardation.

Finally, fragile X syndrome poses a public health dilemma that demands problem solving at the societal level, although just precisely how this should happen remains unclear. Technological advances have now made it possible to screen individuals for either pre- or full mutations of fragile X syndrome, yet even well-informed professionals disagree about who should be screened: all mentally retarded and/or autistic individuals? students with learning disabilities or attention deficits? pregnant women? all newborns? If large-scale testing is accomplished in any one or all of these groups, it remains unclear who should then have access to test results. Further, as noted by Sherman (1992), for screening to be effective, communities will need to ensure that families with the syndrome are not stigmatized, and that supportive services are available, including genetic counseling for at-risk members.

The costs and benefits of large-scale screening programs to society remain uncertain. Are the costs of screening programs justifiable if we lack a specific treatment for fragile X syndrome? Are the costs justified by the probability that some newly identified carriers will choose not to have children, thereby reducing the costs to society of providing long-term care for its mentally retarded citizens? Should these types of cost-benefit analyses even be used to justify screening and treatment programs, or should we, as a society, develop such programs based on shared principles and values? Does society have a role in reviewing the ethical implications of procedures such as preimplantation testing, or are such considerations better left to the individuals who use these novel diagnostic tests?

Solutions to the multiple challenges of fragile X syndrome remain uncertain and open to debate, and are apt to involve differences in opinion among families, professionals, and society at large. Few would disagree, however, that these solutions require both reasoned thought and increased knowledge about this syndrome. It is our hope that this book has provided knowledge about fragile X syndrome that will enable us to approach these unresolved issues in a thoughtful, empathic manner.

REFERENCES

American Psychiatric Association. (1980). *Diagnostic and statistical manual of mental disorders* (3rd ed.). Washington, DC: Author.

American Psychiatric Association. (1987). *Diagnostic and statistical manual of mental disorders* (3rd ed., rev.). Washington, DC: Author.

Anastasi, A. (1972). Four hypotheses and a dearth of data: Response to Lehrke's "A theory of X-linkage of major intellectual traits." *American Journal of Mental Deficiency, 76,* 620-622.

August, G. J., & Lockhart, L. H. (1984). Familial autism and the fragile X chromosome. *Journal of Autism and Developmental Disorders, 14,* 197-204.

Barnett, W. S. (1986). Definition and classification of mental retardation: A reply to Zigler, Balla & Hodapp. *American Journal of Mental Deficiency, 91,* 111-116.

Benezech, M., & Noel, B. (1985). Fra(X) syndrome and autism. *Clinical Genetics, 28,* 93.

Black, S. (1992, June). *Reproductive alternatives for fragile X families.* Paper presented to the Third International Fragile X Conference, Snowmass Resort, CO.

Blomquist, H. K., Bohman, M., Edvinsson, S. O., Gillberg, C., Gustavson, K. H., Holgren, G., & Wahlstrom, J. (1985). Frequency of the fragile X syndrome in infantile autism: A Swedish multicenter study. *Clinical Genetics, 27,* 113-117.

Bolton, P., & Rutter, M. (1989). Females with autism and the fragile X. *Journal of Autism and Developmental Disorders, 19,* 473-476.

Borghgraef, M., Fryns, J. P., Dielkens, A., Pyck, K., & Van den Berghe, H. (1987). Fragile X syndrome: A study of the psychological profile in 23 prepubertal patients. *Clinical Genetics, 32,* 179-186.

Borghgraef, M., Fryns, J. P., & Van den Berghe, H. (1990). The female and the fragile X syndrome: Data on clinical and psychological findings in 7 fragile X carriers. *Clinical Genetics, 37,* 341-346.

Braden, M. L. (1989). *Logo reading system.* (Available from 219 E. St. Vrain, Colorado Springs, CO 80903)

Braden, M. L., & Woods, K. L. (1992). *Logo math-1.* (Available from 219 E. St. Vrain, Colorado Springs, CO 80903)

Brainerd, S. S., Schreiner, R., & Hagerman, R. (1991). Cognitive profiles of carrier fragile X women. *American Journal of Medical Genetics, 38,* 505-508.

Bregman, J. D. (1991). Current developments in the understanding of mental retardation part II: Psychopathology. *Journal of the American Academy of Child and Adolescent Psychiatry, 30,* 861-872.

Bregman, J., Dykens, E. M., Watson, M., Ort, S. I., & Leckman, J. F. (1987). Fragile X syndrome: Variability of phenotypic expression. *Journal of the American Academy of Child and Adolescent Psychiatry, 26,* 461-471.

Bregman, J. D., Leckman, J. F., & Ort, S. I. (1988). Fragile X syndrome: Genetic predisposition to psychopathology. *Journal of Autism and Developmental Disorders, 18,* 343-354.

Bregman, J. D., Leckman, J. F., & Ort, S. I. (1990). Thyroid function in fragile X syndrome males. *Yale Journal of Biology and Medicine, 63,* 293-299.

Brondum-Nielsen, K. (1988). Growth pattern in boys with fragile X syndrome. *American Journal of Medical Genetics, 30,* 143-147.

Brown, F. R., Greer, M. K., Aylward, E. H., & Hunt, H. H. (1990). Intellectual and adaptive functioning in individuals with Down syndrome in relation to age and environmental placement. *Pediatrics, 85,* 450-452.

Brown, W. T., Jenkins, E. C., Cohen, I. L., Fisch, G. S., Wolf-Schein, E. G., Gross, A., Waterhouse, L., Fein, D., Mason-Brothers, A., Ritvo, E., Ruttenberg, B. A., Bentley, W., & Castells, S. (1986). Fragile X syndrome and autism: A multicenter study. *American Journal of Medical Genetics, 23,* 341-352.

Brown, W. T., Jenkins, E. C., Friedman, E., Brooks, J., Cohen, I. L., Duncan, C., Hill, A. L., Malik, M. N., Morris, V., Wolf, E., Wisniewski, K., & French, J. H. (1984). Folic acid therapy in the fragile X syndrome. *American Journal of Medical Genetics, 17,* 289-297.

Brown, W. T., Jenkins, E. C., Friedman, E., Brooks, J., Wisniewski, K., Raguthu, S., & French, J. (1982). Autism is associated with the fragile X syndrome. *Journal of Autism and Developmental Disorders, 12,* 303-307.

Bundey, S., Webb, T., Thake, A., & Todd, J. (1985). A community study of severe mental retardation in the West Midlands and the importance of the fragile X chromosome in its aetiology. *Journal of Medical Genetics, 22,* 258-266.

Butler, M. G., Bruschwig, A., Miller, L. K., & Hagerman, R. J. (1992). Standards for selected anthropometric measurements in males with fragile X syndrome. *Pediatrics, 89,* 1059-1062.

Butler, M. G., Mangrum, T., Gupta, R., & Singh, D. (1991). A 15-item checklist for screening mentally retarded males for the fragile X syndrome. *Clinical Genetics, 39,* 347-354.

Cantu, E. S., Stone, J. W., Wing, A. A., Langee, H. R., & Williams, C. A. (1990). Cytogenetic survey for autistic fragile X carriers in a mental retardation center. *American Journal on Mental Retardation, 94,* 442-447.

Caskey, C. T., Pizzuti, A., Fu, Y.-H., Fenwick, R. G., & Nelson, D. L. (1992). Triplet repeat mutations in human disease. *Science, 256,* 784-789.

Chudley, A. (1984). Behavioral phenotype. In J. Opitz & G. Sutherland (Eds.), Conference report: International Workshop on the Fragile X and X-Linked Mental Retardation. *American Journal of Medical Genetics, 17,* 45-50.

Cianchetti, C., Sannio-Fancello, G., Fratta, A.-L., Manconi, F., Orano, A., Pischedda, M.-P., Pruna, D., Spinicci, G., Archidiacono, N., & Filippi, G. (1991). Neuropsychological, psychiatric, and physical manifestations in 149 members from 18 fragile X families. *American Journal of Medical Genetics, 40,* 234-243.

Cipani, E. (Ed.). (1989). *The treatment of severe behavior disorders: Behavior analysis approaches.* Washington, DC: American Association on Mental Retardation.

104 BEHAVIOR AND DEVELOPMENT IN FRAGILE X SYNDROME

Cohen, I. L., Brown, W. T., Jenkins, E. C., Krawczun, M. S., French, J. H., Raguthu, S., Wolf-Schein, E. G., Sudhalter, V., Fisch, G., & Wisniewski, K. (1989). Fragile X syndrome in autistic females. *American Journal of Medical Genetics, 34,* 302-303.

Cohen, I. L., Fisch, G. S., Sudhalter, V., Wolf-Schein, E. G., Hanson, D., Hagerman, R., Jenkins, E. C., & Brown, W. T. (1988). Social gaze, social avoidance, and repetitive behavior in fragile X males: A controlled study. *American Journal on Mental Retardation, 92,* 436-446.

Cohen, I. L., Sudhalter, V., Pfadt, A., Jenkins, E. C., Brown, W. T., & Vietze, P. M. (1991). Why are autism and the fragile X syndrome associated? Conceptual and methodological issues. *American Journal of Human Genetics, 48,* 195-202.

Cohen, I. L., Vietze, P. M., Sudhalter, V., Jenkins, E. C., & Brown, W. T. (1989). Parent-child dyadic gaze patterns in fragile X males and in non-fragile X males with autistic disorder. *Journal of Child Psychology and Psychiatry, 30,* 845-856.

Cohen, I. L., Vietze, P. M., Sudhalter, V., Jenkins, E. C., & Brown, W. T. (1991). Effects of age and communication level on eye contact in fragile X males and non-fragile X autistic males. *American Journal of Medical Genetics, 38,* 498-502.

Cronister, A., Schreiner, R., Wittenberger, M., Amiri, K., Harris, K., & Hagerman, R. J. (1991). Heterozygous fragile X females: Historical, physical, cognitive and cytogenetic features. *American Journal of Medical Genetics, 28,* 269-274.

Curfs, P. M., Schreppers-Tijdink, G. A., Wiegers, A. M., van Velzen, W., & Fryns, J. P. (1989). Adaptive behavior in the fragile X syndrome: A longitudinal study in eight patients. *American Journal of Medical Genetics, 34,* 502-505.

Das, J. P., Kirby, J., & Jarman, R. F. (1975). Simultaneous and successive abilities: An alternative model for cognitive abilities. *Psychological Bulletin, 82,* 87-103.

Davids, J. R., Hagerman, R. J., & Eilert, R. E. (1990). Orthopaedic aspects of fragile X syndrome. *The Journal of Bone and Joint Surgery, 72-A,* 889-895.

de von Flindt, R., Bybel, B., Chudley, A. E., & Lopes, F. (1991). Short-term memory and cognitive variability in adult fragile X females. *American Journal of Medical Genetics, 38,* 488-492.

Doll, E. A. (1953). *Measurement of social competence: A manual for the Vineland Social Maturity Scale.* Circle Pines, MN: American Guidance Services.

Doll, E. A. (1965). *Vineland Social Maturity Scale.* Circle Pines, MN: American Guidance Services.

Dunn, H. G., Renpenning, H., & Gerrard, J. W. (1963). Mental retardation as a sex-linked defect. *American Journal of Mental Deficiency, 67,* 827-848.

Dunst, C. J. (1990). Sensorimotor development of infants with Down syndrome. In D. Cicchetti & M. Beeghly (Eds.), *Children with Down syndrome: A developmental approach* (pp. 180-230). New York: Cambridge University Press.

Dykens, E. M., Hodapp, R. M., & Evans, D. W. (1992). *Profiles and development of adaptive behavior in children with Down syndrome.* Manuscript submitted for publication.

Dykens, E. M., Hodapp, R. M., & Leckman, J. F. (1987). Strengths and weaknesses in the intellectual functioning of males with fragile X syndrome. *American Journal of Mental Deficiency, 92,* 234-236.

Dykens, E. M., Hodapp, R. M., & Leckman, J. F. (1989). Adaptive and maladaptive functioning of institutionalized and noninstitutionalized males with fragile X syndrome. *Journal of the American Academy of Child and Adolescent Psychiatry, 28,* 427-430.

Dykens, E. M., Hodapp, R. M., Ort, S. I., Finucane, B., Shapiro, L., & Leckman, J. F. (1989). The trajectory of cognitive development in males with fragile X syndrome. *Journal of the American Academy of Child and Adolescent Psychiatry, 28,* 422-428.

Dykens, E. M., Hodapp, R. M., Ort, S. I., & Leckman, J. F. (1992). *Profiles of adaptive behavior in fragile X syndrome, Down syndrome and nonretarded males.* Manuscript submitted for publication.

Dykens, E. M., Hodapp, R. M., Ort, S. I., & Leckman, J. F. (1993). Trajectory of adaptive behavior in males with fragile X syndrome. *Journal of Autism and Developmental Disorders, 23,* 135-145.

Dykens, E. M., Hodapp, R. M., Walsh, K., & Nash, L. J. (1992a). Adaptive and maladaptive behavior in Prader-Willi syndrome. *Journal of the American Academy of Child and Adolescent Psychiatry, 31,* 1131-1136.

Dykens, E. M., Hodapp, R. M., Walsh, K., & Nash, L. J. (1992b). Profiles, correlates and trajectories of intelligence in Prader-Willi syndrome. *Journal of the American Academy of Child and Adolescent Psychiatry, 31,* 1125-1130.

Dykens, E. M., & Leckman, J. F. (1990). Developmental issues in fragile X syndrome. In R. M. Hodapp, J. A. Burack, & E. Zigler (Eds.), *Issues in the developmental approach to mental retardation* (pp. 226-245). New York: Cambridge University Press.

Dykens, E. M., Leckman, J. F., Paul, R., & Watson, M. (1988). Cognitive, behavioral, and adaptive functioning in fragile X and non-fragile X retarded men. *Journal of Autism and Developmental Disorders, 18,* 41-52.

Dykens, E. M., Leckman, J. F., Riddle, M., Hardin, M., Schwartz, S., & Cohen, D. J. (1991). Intellectual and adaptive functioning of Tourette syndrome children with and without hyperactivity. *Journal of Abnormal Child Psychology, 18,* 607-615.

Dykens, E. M., Volkmar, F., & Glick, M. (1991). Thought disorder in high functioning autistic adults. *Journal of Autism and Developmental Disorders, 21,* 291-301.

Einfeld, S. L. (1988). Autism and the fragile X syndrome [Letter to the editor]. *American Journal of Medical Genetics, 30,* 237-238.

Einfeld, S. L., Hall, W., & Levy, F. (1991). Hyperactivity and fragile X syndrome. *Journal of Abnormal Child Psychology, 19,* 253-262.

Einfeld, S. L., Molony, H., & Hall, W. (1989). Autism is not associated with the fragile X syndrome. *American Journal of Medical Genetics, 34,* 187-193.

Eyman, R. K., & Arndt, S. (1982). Life-span development of institutionalized and community-based mentally retarded residents. *American Journal of Mental Deficiency, 86,* 342-350.

Ferrier, L. J., Bashir, A. S., Meryash, D. L., Johnston, J., & Wolff, P. (1991). Conversational skills of individuals with fragile-X syndrome: A comparison with autism and Down syndrome. *Developmental Medicine and Child Neurology, 33,* 766-788.

Finucane, B., Kurtz, M. B., & Scott, C. I. (1992). New mental retardation syndrome with hearing impairment, distinct facial appearance, and skeletal anomalies. *American Journal of Medical Genetics, 43,* 844-847.

Fisch, G. S. (1992). Is autism associated with the fragile X syndrome? *American Journal of Medical Genetics, 43,* 47-55.

Fisch, G. S., Ariname, T., Froster-Iskenius, U., Fryns, J. P., Curfs, L. M., Borghgraef, M., Howard-Peebles, P. N., Schwartz, C. E., Simensen, R. G., & Shapiro, L. R. (1991). Relationship between age and IQ among fragile X males: A multicenter study. *American Journal of Medical Genetics, 38,* 481-487.

Fisch, G. S., Cohen, I. L., Jenkins, E. C., & Brown, W. T. (1988). Screening developmentally disabled male populations for the fragile X syndrome: The effect of sample size. *American Journal of Medical Genetics, 30,* 655-663.

Fisch, G. S., Cohen, I. L., Wolf, E. G., Brown, W. T., Jenkins, E. C., & Gross, A. (1986). Autism and the fragile X syndrome. *American Journal of Psychiatry, 143,* 71-73.

Fowler, A. (1988). Determinants of rate of language growth in children with Down syndrome. In L. Nadel (Ed.), *The psychobiology of Down syndrome* (pp. 217-245). Cambridge: MIT Press.

Fowler, A. (1990). The development of language structure in children with Down syndrome: Evidence for a specific syntactic delay. In D. Cicchetti & M. Beeghly (Eds.), *Children with Down syndrome: A developmental approach* (pp. 302-328). New York: Cambridge University Press.

Freund, L. S., & Baumgardner, T. (1992, June). *WISC-R profile and neuropsychological function in girls with fragile X.* Paper presented at the Third International Fragile X Conference, Snowmass Resort, CO.

Freund, L. S., Reiss, A. L., Hagerman, R. J., & Vinogradov, S. (1992). Chromosome fragility and psychopathology in obligate female carriers of the fragile X chromosome. *Archives of General Psychiatry, 49,* 54-60.

Frith, U., & Baron-Cohen, S. (1987). Perception in autistic children. In D. J. Cohen, A. M. Donnellan, & R. Paul (Eds.), *Handbook of autism and developmental disorders* (pp. 85-102). New York, NY: John Wiley.

Fryns, J. P. (1986). The female and the fragile X: A study of 144 obligate female carriers. *American Journal of Medical Genetics, 23,* 157-169.

Fryns, J. P., Jacobs, J., Kleczkowska, A., & Van den Berghe, H. (1984). The psychological profile of the fragile X syndrome. *Clinical Genetics, 25,* 131-134.

Fryns, J. P., Moerman, P., Gilis, D., d'Espallier, L., & Van den Berghe, H. (1988). Suggestively increased rate of infant death in children of fragile X positive mothers. *American Journal of Medical Genetics, 30,* 252-265.

Fryns, J. P., & Van den Berghe, H. (1983). X-linked mental retardation and fragile Xq27 site. *Clinical Genetics, 23,* 203-206.

Fu, Y.-H., Kuhl, D. P., Pizzuti, A., Sutcliffe, J. S., Richards, S., Verkerk, A. J., Holden, J. A., Fenwick, R. G., Warren, S. T., Oostra, B. A., Nelson, D. L., & Caskey, C. T. (1991). Variation of the CGG repeat at the fragile site results in genetic instability: Resolution of the Sherman paradox. *Cell, 67,* 1047-1058.

Fu, Y.-H., Ranjnarayan, S., Dunne, D. W., Dubel, J., Nasser, G. A., Ashizawa, T., De Jong, P., et al. (1992). An unstable triplet repeat in a gene related to myotonic dystrophy. *Science, 255,* 1256-1258.

Gibson, D. (1966). Early developmental staging as a prophesy index in Down's syndrome. *American Journal of Mental Deficiency, 70,* 825-828.

Gillberg, C., Ohlson, V., Wahlstrom, J., Steffenburg, S., & Blix, K. (1988). Monozygotic female twins with autism and the fragile X syndrome (AFRAX). *Journal of Child Psychology and Psychiatry, 29,* 447-451.

Gillberg, C., Persson, E., & Wahlstom, J. (1986). The autism fragile X syndrome (AFRAX): A population based study of ten boys. *Journal of Mental Deficiency Research, 30,* 27-39.

Gillberg, C., Steffenburg, S., & Jakobsson, G. (1987). Neurobiological findings in 20 relatively gifted children with Kanner-type autism or Asperger syndrome. *Developmental Medicine and Child Neurology, 29,* 641-649.

Gillberg, C., & Wahlstrom, J. (1985). Chromosome abnormalities in infantile autism and other childhood psychoses: A population study of 66 cases. *Developmental Medicine and Child Neurology, 27,* 293-304.

Goldberg, S., Marcovitch, S., MacGregor, D., & Lojkasek, M. (1986). Family responses to developmentally delayed preschoolers: Etiology and the father's role. *American Journal of Mental Deficiency, 90,* 610-617.

Goldfine, P. E., McPherson, P. M., Heath, G. A., Hardesty, V. A., Beauregard, L. J., & Gordon, B. (1985). Association of fragile X syndrome with autism. *American Journal of Psychiatry, 142,* 108-110.

Goldman-Rakic, P. (1987). Development of cortical circuitry and cognitive function. *Child Development, 58,* 601-622.

Grigsby, J. P., Kemper, M. B., Hagerman, R. J., & Myers, C. S. (1990). Neuropsychological dysfunction among affected heterozygous fragile X females. *American Journal of Medical Genetics, 35,* 28-35.

Grossman, H. J. (Ed.). (1983). *Classification in mental retardation* (rev. ed.). Washington, DC: American Association on Mental Deficiency.

Gustavson, K. H., Blomquist, H. K., & Holgren, G. (1986). Prevalence of the fragile X syndrome in mentally retarded children in a Swedish county. *American Journal of Medical Genetics, 23,* 581-587.

Hagerman, R. J. (1987). Fragile X syndrome. *Current Problems in Pediatrics,* 627-673.

Hagerman, R. J. (1989). Behavior and treatment of the fragile X syndrome. In K. E. Davies (Ed.), *The fragile X syndrome* (pp. 56-75). New York: Oxford University Press.

Hagerman, R. J. (1991). Physical and behavioral phenotype. In R. J. Hagerman & A. C. Silverman (Eds.), *Fragile X syndrome: Diagnosis, treatment and research* (pp. 3-67). Baltimore, MD: Johns Hopkins University Press.

Hagerman, R. J., Altshul-Stark, D., & McBogg, P. (1987). Recurrent otitis media in the fragile X syndrome. *American Journal of Diseases in Children, 141,* 184-187.

Hagerman, R. J., Amiri, K., & Cronister, A. (1991). Fragile X checklist. *American Journal of Medical Genetics, 38,* 283-287.

Hagerman, R. J., Chudley, A. E., Knoll, J. H., Jackson, A. W., Kemper, M., & Ahmad, R. (1986). Autism in fragile X females. *American Journal of Medical Genetics, 23,* 375-380.

Hagerman, R. J., Jackson, C., Amiri, K., Silverman, A. C., O'Connor, R., & Sobesky, W. (1992). Girls with fragile X syndrome: Physical and neurocognitive status and outcome. *Pediatrics, 89,* 395-400.

Hagerman, R. J., Jackson, A. W., Levitas, A., Rimland, B., & Braden, M. (1986). An analysis of autism in fifty males with the fragile X syndrome. *American Journal of Medical Genetics, 23,* 359-374.

Hagerman, R. J., Kemper, M., & Hudson, M. (1985). Learning disabilities and attentional problems in boys with the fragile X syndrome. *American Journal of Diseases in Children, 139,* 674-678.

Hagerman, R. J., Levitas, A., & Rogers, S. (1992, June). *Autism and schizophrenia: Identification and treatment of psychosis in fragile X.* Paper presented at the Third International Fragile X Conference, Snowmass Resort, CO.

Hagerman, R. J., Murphy, M. A., & Wittenberger, M. D. (1988). A controlled trial of stimulant medication in children with the fragile X syndrome. *American Journal of Medical Genetics, 30,* 377-392.

Hagerman, R. J., Schreiner, R. A., Kemper, M., Wittenberger, M. D., Zahn, M., & Habicht, K. (1989). Longitudinal IQ changes in fragile X males. *American Journal of Medical Genetics, 33,* 513-518.

Hagerman, R. J., Smith, A. C., & Mariner, R. (1983). Clinical features of the fragile X syndrome. In R. J. Hagerman & P. K. McBogg (Eds.), *The fragile X syndrome: Diagnosis, biochemistry, intervention,* (pp. 17-53). Dillon, CO: Spectra.

Hagerman, R. J., & Sobesky, W. E. (1989). Psychopathology in fragile X syndrome. *American Journal of Orthopsychiatry, 59,* 142-152.

Hall, W., & Einfeld, S. (1990). On doing the "impossible": Inferring that a putative causal relationship does not exist. *Australian and New Zealand Journal of Psychiatry, 24,* 217-226.

Hanson, D. M., Jackson, A., & Hagerman, R. (1986). Speech disturbances (cluttering) in mildly impaired males with the Martin-Bell/Fragile X syndrome. *American Journal of Medical Genetics, 23,* 195-206.

Harpey, J. P. (1982). Treatment of fragile X. *Pediatrics, 69,* 670.

Harvey, J., Judge, C., & Weiner, S. (1976). Familial X-linked mental retardation with an X chromosome abnormality. *Journal of Medical Genetics, 14,* 46-50.

Hecht, F. (1991). Seizure disorders in the fragile X chromosome disorder. *American Journal of Medical Genetics, 38,* 509.

Herbst, D. S., Dunn, H. G., Dill, F. J., Kalousek, D. K., & Krywaniuk, L. W. (1981). Further delineation of X-linked mental retardation. *Human Genetics, 58,* 366-371.

Herbst, D. S., & Miller, J. R. (1980). Nonspecific mental retardation. II. The frequency in British Columbia. *American Journal of Medical Genetics, 7,* 461-469.

Hinton, G. (1991). *Rebus primer.* (Available from Mesa Micro, 630 North Windsor, Mesa, AZ 85213-6811)

Hinton, V. J., Dobkin, C. S., Halperin, J. M., Jenkins, E. C., Brown, W. T., Ding, X. H., Cohen, I. L., Rousseau, F., & Miezejeski, C. M. (1992). Mode of inheritance influences behavioral expression and molecular control of cognitive deficits in female carriers of the fragile X syndrome. *American Journal of Medical Genetics, 43,* 87-95.

Ho, H. H., & Kalousek, D. K. (1989). Fragile X syndrome in autistic boys. *Journal of Autism and Developmental Disorders, 19,* 343-347.

Ho, H. H., Glahn, T. J., & Ho, J. C. (1988). The fragile X syndrome. *Developmental Medicine and Child Neurology, 30,* 252-265.

Hockey, A., & Crowhurst, J. (1988). Early manifestations of the Martin-Bell syndrome based on a series of both sexes from infancy. *American Journal of Medical Genetics, 30,* 61-71.

Hodapp, R. M., & Burack, J. A. (1990). What mental retardation tells us about typical development: The examples of sequences, rates, and cross-domain relations. *Development and Psychopathology, 2,* 213-226.

Hodapp, R. M., & Dykens, E. M. (1991). Toward an etiology-specific strategy of early intervention with handicapped children. In K. Marfo (Ed.), *Early intervention in transition: Current perspectives on programs for handicapped children* (pp. 41-60). New York: Praeger.

Hodapp, R. M., & Dykens, E. M. (1992). The role of etiology in the education of children with mental retardation. *McGill Journal of Education, 27,* 165-173.

Hodapp, R. M., & Dykens, E. M. (in press). Mental retardation's two cultures of behavioral research. *American Journal on Mental Retardation.*

Hodapp, R. M., Dykens, E. M., Evans, D. W., & Merighi, J. R. (1992). Maternal emotional reactions to young children with different types of handicaps. *Developmental and Behavioral Pediatrics, 13,* 118-123.

Hodapp, R. M., Dykens, E. M., Hagerman, R. J., Schreiner, R., Lachiewicz, A., & Leckman, J. F. (1990). Developmental implications of changing trajectories of IQ in males with fragile X syndrome. *Journal of the American Academy of Child and Adolescent Psychiatry, 29,* 214-219.

Hodapp, R. M., Dykens, E. M., Ort, S. I., Zelinsky, D. R., & Leckman, J. F. (1991). Changing patterns of intellectual strengths and weaknesses in males with fragile X syndrome. *Journal of Autism and Developmental Disorders, 21,* 503-516.

Hodapp, R. M., Leckman, J. F., Dykens, E. M., Sparrow, S., Zelinsky, D., & Ort, S. (1992). K-ABC profiles in children with fragile X syndrome, Down syndrome, and nonspecific mental retardation. *American Journal on Mental Retardation, 97,* 39-46.

Hodapp, R. M., & Zigler, E. (1990). Applying the developmental perspective to individuals with Down syndrome. In D. Cicchetti & M. Beeghly (Eds.), *Children with Down syndrome: A developmental perspective* (pp. 1-28). New York: Cambridge University Press.

Holroyd, J., & MacArthur, D. (1978). Mental retardation and stress on the parents: A contrast between Down syndrome and childhood autism. *American Journal of Mental Deficiency, 80,* 431-436.

Howard-Peebles, P., Stoddard, G., & Mims, M. (1979). Familial X-linked mental retardation, verbal disability, and marker X chromosomes. *American Journal of Human Genetics, 31,* 214-222.

Hurley, A. D. (1989). Individual psychotherapy with mentally retarded individuals: A review and call for research. *Research in Developmental Disabilities, 10,* 261-275.

Jacobs, P. A., Mayer, M., Matsuura, J., Rhoads, F., & Yee, S. C. (1983). A cytogenetic study of a population of mentally retarded males with special reference to the marker (X) syndrome. *Human Genetics, 63,* 139-148.

Jacobson, J. W. (1982). Problem behavior and psychiatric impairment within a developmentally disabled population: I. Behavior frequency. *Applied Research in Mental Retardation, 3,* 121-139.

Jacobson, J. W. (1990). Do some mental disorders occur less frequently among persons with mental retardation? *American Journal on Mental Retardation, 94,* 596-602.

Jorgensen, O. S., Nielsen, K. B., Isager, T., & Mouridsen, S. E. (1984). Fragile X-chromosome among child psychiatric patients with disturbances of language and social relationships. *Acta Psychiatrica Scandinavica, 70,* 510-514.

Kaufman, A. S., & Kaufman, N. L. (1983). *Kaufman Assessment Battery for Children.* Circle Pines, MN: American Guidance Service.

Kemper, M. B., Hagerman, R. J., & Altshul-Stark, D. (1988). Cognitive profiles of boys with fragile X syndrome. *American Journal of Medical Genetics, 30,* 191-200.

Kerbeshian, J., Burd, L., & Martsolf, J. T. (1984). Fragile X syndrome associated with Tourette symptomatology in a male with moderate mental retardation and autism. *Developmental and Behavioral Pediatrics, 5,* 201-203.

Kirkilionis, A. J., Pozsonyi, J., & Sergovich, F. R. (1988). The use of testicular volume as a clinical marker for cytogenetic disorders in mentally retarded males. *Journal of Mental Deficiency Research, 32,* 19-30.

Krauss, M. W., & Seltzer, M. M. (1986). Comparison of elderly and adult mentally retarded persons in community and institutional settings. *American Journal of Mental Deficiency, 91,* 237-243.

Lachiewicz, A. M. (1992a). Abnormal behavior of young girls with fragile X syndrome. *American Journal of Medical Genetics, 43,* 72-77.

Lachiewicz, A. M. (1992b, June). *Distinguishing physical features of boys with fragile X syndrome.* Paper presented to the Third International Fragile X Conference, Snowmass Resort, CO.

Lachiewicz, A. M., Gullion, C., Spiridigliozzi, G., & Aylsworth, A. (1987). Declining IQs of young males with fragile X syndrome. *American Journal on Mental Retardation, 92,* 272-278.

Landesman-Dwyer, S., & Sulzbacher, F. (1981). Residential placement and adaptation of severely and profoundly retarded individuals. In R. Bruininks, C. Meyers, C. Stiedard, & K. Lakin (Eds.), *Deinstitutionalization and community adjustment of mentally retarded people* (pp. 182-194). Washington, DC: American Association on Mental Deficiency.

Largo, R. H., & Schinzel, A. (1985). Developmental and behavioral disturbances in 13 boys with fragile X syndrome. *European Journal of Pediatrics, 143,* 269-275.

Leckman, J. F. (1987, December). *Medications in fragile X children.* Paper presented to the First National Fragile X Conference, Denver, CO.

Lehrke, R. G. (1972). A theory of X-linkage of major intellectual traits. *American Journal of Mental Deficiency, 76,* 611-619.

Lehrke, R. G. (1974). X-linked mental retardation and verbal ability. *Birth Defects: Original Article Series, 10,* 1-100.

Lejune, J. (1982, January 30). Is the fragile X syndrome amenable to treatment? *The Lancet,* 273-274.

Levinson, G., Maddalena, A., Howard-Peebles, P. N., Black, S. H., Fugger, E. F., Palmer, F. T., Harton, G. L., Fields, R., Neel, B. L., Clifford, N. D., & Schulman, J. D. (1992, June). *Preimplantation genetic screening: An option for families at risk for transmission of the fragile X chromosome.* Poster presentation to the Third International Fragile X Conference, Snowmass Resort, CO.

Levitas, A., Hagerman, R. J., Braden, M., Rimland, B., McBogg, P., & Matus, I. (1983). Autism and the fragile X syndrome. *Developmental and Behavioral Pediatrics, 4,* 151-158.

Loehr, J. P., Synhorst, D. P., Wolfe, R. R., & Hagerman, R. J. (1986). Aortic root dilatation and mitral valve prolapse in the fragile X syndrome. *American Journal of Medical Genetics, 23,* 189-194.

Loesch, D. Z., & Hay, D. A. (1988). Clinical features and reproductive patterns in fragile X female heterozygotes. *Journal of Medical Genetics, 25,* 407-414.

Loesch, D. Z., Lafranchi, M., & Scott, D. (1988). Anthropometry in Martin-Bell syndrome. *American Journal of Medical Genetics, 30,* 149-164.

Loveland, K. A., & Kelly, M. L. (1988). Development of adaptive behavior in adolescents and adults with autism and Down syndrome. *American Journal on Mental Retardation, 93,* 84-92.

Lubs, H. A. (1969). A marker X chromosome. *American Journal of Human Genetics, 21,* 231-244.

Luckasson, R., Coulter, D. L., Polloway, E., Reiss, S., Schalock, R. L., Snell, M. E., Spitalnik, D. M., & Stark, J. A. (1992). *Definition and classification in mental retardation* (9th ed.). Washington, DC: American Association on Mental Retardation.

Madison, L. S., George, C., & Moeschler, J. B. (1986). Cognitive functioning in the fragile-X syndrome: A study of intellectual, memory, and communication skills. *Journal of Mental Deficiency Research, 30,* 129-148.

Maino, D. M., Wesson, M., Schlange, D., Cibis, G., & Maino, J. H. (1991). Optometric findings in the fragile X syndrome. *Optometry and Vision Science, 68,* 634-640.

Marans, W., Paul, R., & Leckman, J. (1987). *Speech and language profiles in males with fragile X syndrome.* Paper presented at the American Speech and Hearing Association Convention, New Orleans.

Martin, J. P., & Bell, J. (1943). A pedigree of mental defect showing sex-linkage. *Journal of Neurological Psychiatry, 6,* 154-157.

Matson, J. L., & Gorman-Smith, D. (1986). A review of treatment research for aggressive and disruptive behavior in the mentally retarded. *Applied Research in Mental Retardation, 7,* 95-103.

Mazzocco, M. M., Hagerman, R. J., Cronister-Silverman, A., & Pennington, B. F. (1992). Specific frontal lobe deficits among women with the fragile X gene. *Journal of the American Academy of Child and Adolescent Psychiatry, 31,* 1141-1148.

McGillivray, B. C., Herbst, D. S., Dill, F. J., Sandercock, H. J., & Tischler, B. (1986). Infantile autism: An occasional manifestation of fragile X mental retardation. *American Journal of Medical Genetics, 23,* 353-358.

Mendlewicz, J., & Hirsch, D. (1991). Bipolar manic depressive illness and the fragile X syndrome. *Biological Psychiatry, 29,* 298-299.

Meryash, D. L. (1989). Perception of burden among at-risk women of raising a child with fragile-X syndrome. *Clinical Genetics, 36,* 15-24.

Meryash, D. L. (1992). Characteristics of fragile X relatives with different attitudes toward terminating an affected pregnancy. *American Journal on Mental Retardation, 96,* 528-535.

Meryash, D. L., & Abuelo, D. (1988). Counseling needs and attitudes toward prenatal diagnosis and abortion in fragile X families. *Clinical Genetics, 33,* 349-355.

Meryash, D. L., Szymanski, L. S., & Gerald, P. (1982). Infantile autism associated with the fragile X syndrome. *Journal of Autism and Developmental Disorders, 12,* 295-296.

Miezejeski, C. M., Jenkins, E. C., Hill, A. L., Wisniewski, K., French, J. H., & Brown, W. T. (1986). A profile of cognitive deficit in females from fragile X families. *Neuropsychologia, 24,* 405-409.

Miller, J., & Chapman, R. (1984). Disorders of communication: Investigating the development of language of mentally retarded children. *American Journal of Mental Deficiency, 88,* 536-545.

Minnes, P. M. (1988). Family stress associated with a developmentally handicapped child. *International Review of Research in Mental Retardation, 15,* 195-226.

Musumeci, S. A., Ferri, R., Colognola, R. M., Neri, G., Sanfilippo, S., & Bergonzi, P. (1988). Prevalence of a novel epileptogenic EEG pattern in the Martin-Bell syndrome. *American Journal of Medical Genetics, 30,* 207-212.

Musumeci, S. A., Ferri, R., Elia, M., Colognola, R. M., Bergonzi, P., & Tassinari, C. A. (1991). Epilepsy and fragile X syndrome: A follow-up study. *American Journal of Medical Genetics, 38,* 511-513.

Naglieri, J. A. (1985). Use of the WISC-R and K-ABC with learning disabled, borderline mentally retarded, and normal children. *Psychology in the Schools, 22,* 133-141.

Newell, K., Sanborn, B., & Hagerman, R. (1983). Speech and language dysfunction in the fragile X syndrome. In R. J. Hagerman & P. M. McBogg (Eds.), *The fragile X syndrome: Diagnosis, biochemistry, and intervention* (pp. 175-200). Dillon, CO: Spectra.

Nielsen, K. B. (1983). Diagnosis of the fragile X syndrome (Martin Bell syndrome). Clinical findings in 27 males with the fragile site at Xq28. *Journal of Mental Deficiency Research, 27,* 211-226.

Oberlé, I., Rousseau, F., Heitz, D., Kretz, C., Devys, D., Hanauer, A., Boue, J., Bertheas, M. F., & Mandel, J. L. (1991). Instability of a 550-base pair DNA segment and abnormal methylation in fragile X syndrome. *Science, 252,* 1097-1110.

Obrzut, A., Nelson, R. B., & Obrzut, J. E. (1987). Construct validity of the Kaufman Assessment Battery for Children with mildly mentally retarded students. *American Journal of Mental Deficiency, 92,* 74-77.

Opitz, J. M. (1986). On the gates of hell and a most unusual gene. *American Journal of Medical Genetics, 23,* 1-10.

Opitz, J. M. (1987). Erratum. *American Journal of Medical Genetics, 26,* 37.

Opitz, J. M., Segal, A. T., Klove, H., Mathews, C., & Lehrke, R. G. (1965). X-linked mental retardation: Study of a large kindred with 20 affected members. *Journal of Pediatrics, 67,* 713-714.

Opitz, J. M., Westphal, J. M., & Daniel, A. (1984). Discovery of a connective tissue dysplasia in the Martin-Bell syndrome. *American Journal of Medical Genetics, 17,* 101-109.

Partington, M. W. (1984). The fragile X syndrome II: Preliminary data on growth and development in males. *American Journal of Medical Genetics, 17,* 175-194.

Partington, M. W. (1988). Female relatives with the fragile X syndrome. *American Journal of Medical Genetics, 23,* 111-126.

Paul, R. (1987). Communication. In D. J. Cohen, A. M. Donnellan, & R. Paul (Eds.), *Handbook of autism and pervasive developmental disorders* (pp. 61-84). New York: John Wiley.

Paul, R., Cohen, D., Breg, R., Watson, M., & Herman, S. (1984). Fragile X syndrome: Its relations to speech and language disorders. *Journal of Speech and Hearing Disorders, 49,* 326-336.

Paul, R., Dykens, E., Leckman, J. F., Watson, M., Breg, R. W., & Cohen, D. J. (1987). A comparison of language characteristics of mentally retarded adults with fragile X syndrome and those with nonspecific mental retardation and autism. *Journal of Autism and Developmental Disorders, 17,* 457-468.

Payton, J. B., Steele, M. W., Wenger, S. L., & Minshew, N. J. (1989). The fragile X marker and autism in perspective. *Journal of the American Academy of Child and Adolescent Psychiatry, 28,* 417-421.

Pecile, V., & Filippi, G. (1991). Screening for fragile X mutation and Klinefelter syndrome in mental institutions. *Clinical Genetics, 39,* 189-193.

Pennington, B., O'Connor, R. A., & Sudhalter, V. (1991). Toward a neuropsychology of fragile X syndrome. In R. J. Hagerman & A. C. Silverman (Eds.), *Fragile X syndrome: Diagnosis, treatment, and research* (pp. 173-201). Baltimore, MD: Johns Hopkins University Press.

Pergolizzi, R. G., Erster, S. H., Goonewardena, P., & Brown, W. T. (1992). Detection of the full fragile X mutation. *Lancet, 399,* 271-272.

Pieretti, M., Zhang, F., Fu, Y.-H., Warren, S. T., Oostra, B. A., Caskey, C. T., & Nelson, D. L. (1991). Absence of expression of the FMR-1 gene in fragile X syndrome. *Cell, 66*, 817-822.

Pueschel, S. M., Gallagher, P. L., Zartler, A. S., & Pezzullo, J. C. (1987). Cognitive and learning processes in children with Down syndrome. *Research in Developmental Disabilities, 8*, 21-37.

Pueschel, S. M., Herman, R., & Groden, G. (1985). Screening children with autism for fragile X syndrome and phenylketonuria. *Journal of Autism and Developmental Disorders, 15*, 335-338.

Reiss, A. L. (1988). Vernal lobules VI and VII in fragile X syndrome. *New England Journal of Medicine, 319*, 1152-1153.

Reiss, A. L. (1992, June). *Neuroimaging in fragile X males and females.* Paper presented to the Third International Fragile X Conference, Snowmass Resort, CO.

Reiss, A. L., Aylward, E., Freund, L. S., Joshi, P. K., & Bryan, R. N. (1991). Neuroanatomy of the fragile X syndrome: The posterior fossa. *Annals of Neurology, 29*, 26-32.

Reiss, A. L., Cianchetti, C., Cohen, I. L., DeVries, B., Hagerman, R., Hinton, V., Froster, U., Lachiewicz, A., Mazzocco, M., Sobesky, W., & Sudhalter, V. (1992). Brief screening questionnaire for determining affected state in fragile X syndrome: A consensus recommendation. *American Journal of Medical Genetics, 43*, 61-64.

Reiss, A. L., Feinstein, C., Toomey, K. E., Goldsmith, B., Rosenbaum, K., & Caruso, M. A. (1986). Psychiatric disability associated with the fragile X chromosome. *American Journal of Medical Genetics, 23*, 393-401.

Reiss, A. L., & Freund, L. (1990). Fragile X syndrome, DSM-III-R, and autism. *Journal of the American Academy of Child and Adolescent Psychiatry, 29*, 885-891.

Reiss, A. L., & Freund, L. (1992). Behavioral phenotype of fragile X syndrome: DSM-III-R autistic behavior in male children. *American Journal of Medical Genetics, 43*, 35-46.

Reiss, A. L., Freund, L., Vinogradov, S., Hagerman, R. J., & Cronister, A. (1989). Parental inheritance and psychological disability in fragile X females. *American Journal of Human Genetics, 45*, 697-705.

Reiss, A. L., Hagerman, R. J., Vinogradov, S., Abrams, M., & King, R. J. (1988). Psychiatric disability in female carriers of the fragile X chromosome. *Archives of General Psychiatry, 45*, 25-30.

Rhoads, F. A. (1984). Fragile-X syndrome in Hawaii: A summary of clinical experience. *American Journal of Medical Genetics, 17*, 209-214.

Rodewald, A., Froster-Iskenius, U., Kab, E., Langenbeck, U., Schnizel, A., Schmidt, A., Schwinger, E., Stembech, P., Veenema, T. T., Wegner, D., Wirtz, A., Zankl, H., & Zankl, M. (1986). Dermatoglyphic peculiarities in families with X-linked mental retardation at the fragile site Xq27: A collaborative study. *Clinical Genetics, 30*, 1-13.

Rosenblatt, D. S., Duschenes, E. A., Hellstrom, F. V., Golick, M. S., Vekemans, M. J., Zeesman, S. F., & Andermann, A. (1985). Folic acid blinded trial in identical twins with fragile X syndrome. *American Journal of Human Genetics, 37*, 543-552.

Ross, R., Begab, M., Dondis, E., Giampiccolo, J., & Meyers, C. (1985). *Lives of the mentally retarded: A forty year follow-up study.* Stanford, CA: Stanford University Press.

Rowitz, L. (1988). Homogenization of deviance. *Mental Retardation, 26*, 1-3.

Rutter, M., Macdonald, H., Le Couteur, A., Harrington, R., Bolton, P., & Bailey, A. (1990). Genetic factors in child psychiatric disorders—II. Empirical findings. *Journal of Child Psychology and Psychiatry, 31,* 39-83.

Scarr, S., & Weinberg, R. A. (1978). The influence of family background on intellectual attainment. *American Sociological Review, 43,* 642-692.

Scharfenaker, S., Hickman, L., & Braden, M. (1991). An integrated approach to intervention. In R. J. Hagerman & A. C. Silverman (Eds.), *Fragile X syndrome: Diagnosis, treatment and research* (pp. 327-372). Baltimore, MD: Johns Hopkins University Press.

Shapiro, L. R. (1991). The fragile X syndrome: A peculiar pattern of inheritance. *New England Journal of Medicine, 325,* 1736-1738.

Sherman, S. (1992, June). *Epidemiology and screening.* Paper presented at the Third International Fragile X Conference, Snowmass Resort, CO.

Sherman, S. L., Jacobs, P. A., Morton, N. E., Froster-Iskenius, U., Howard-Peebles, P. N., Brondum-Nielson, K., Partington, M. W., Sutherland, G. R., Turner, G., & Watson, M. (1985). Further segregation analysis of the fra(X) syndrome with special reference to transmitting males. *American Journal of Human Genetics, 69,* 389-399.

Sherman, S. L., Morton, N. E., Jacobs, P. A., & Turner, G. (1984). The marker (X) syndrome: Cytogenetic and genetic analysis. *Annals of Human Genetics, 48,* 21-37.

Silverstein, A. B. (1982). A note on the constancy of IQ. *American Journal of Mental Deficiency, 87,* 227-229.

Silverstein, A. B., Herbs, D., Miller, T. J., Nasuta, R., Williams, D. L., & White, J. F. (1988). Effects of age on the adaptive behavior of institutionalized and non-institutionalized individuals with Down syndrome. *American Journal of Mental Deficiency, 92,* 455-460.

Simensen, R. J., & Rogers, R. C. (1989). Fragile X syndrome. *American Family Physician, 39,* 185-192.

Simko, A., Hornstein, L., Soukup, S., & Bagamery, N. (1989). Fragile X syndrome: Recognition in young children. *Pediatrics, 83,* 547-552.

Simpson, N. E. (1986). Dermatoglyphic indices of males with the fragile X syndrome and of the female heterozygote. *American Journal of Medical Genetics, 23,* 171-178.

Simpson, N. E., Newman, B. J., & Partington, M. W. (1984). Fragile X syndrome: III. Dermatoglyphic studies in males. *American Journal of Medical Genetics, 17,* 195-207.

Sobesky, W. (1992, June). *The emotional phenotype in mildly affected carriers.* Paper presented at the Third International Fragile X Conference, Snowmass Resort, CO.

Solnit, A., & Stark, M. (1961). Mourning and the birth of a defective child. *Psychoanalytic Study of the Child, 16,* 523-537.

Sovner, R. (1989). The use of valproate in the treatment of mentally retarded persons with typical and atypical bipolar disorders. *Journal of Clinical Psychiatry, 50,* 40-43.

Sparrow, S. S., Balla, D., & Cicchetti, D. (1984). *Vineland Adaptive Behavior Scales.* Circle Pines, MN: American Guidance Service.

Sreeram, N., Wren, C., Bhate, M., Robertson, P., & Hunter, S. (1989). Cardiac abnormalities in the fragile X syndrome. *British Heart Journal, 61,* 289-291.

Steyaert, J., Borghgraef, M., Gaulthier, C., Fryns, J. P., & Van den Berghe, H. (1992). Cognitive profile in adult, normal intelligence female fragile X carriers. *American Journal of Medical Genetics, 43,* 116-119.

Storm, R. L., PeBenito, R., & Ferretti, C. (1987). Ophthalmologic findings in the fragile X syndrome. *Archives of Ophthalmology, 105,* 1099-1102.

Sudhalter, V., Cohen, I., Silverman, W., & Wolf-Schein, E. (1990). Conversational analyses of males with fragile X, Down syndrome and autism: Comparison of the emergence of deviant language. *American Journal on Mental Retardation, 94*, 431-441.

Sudhalter, V., Maranion, M., & Brooks, P. (1992). Expressive semantic deficit in the productive language of males with fragile X syndrome. *American Journal of Medical Genetics, 43*, 65-71.

Sudhalter, V., Scarborough, H., & Cohen, I. (1991). Syntactic delay and pragmatic deviance in the language of fragile X males. *American Journal of Medical Genetics, 38*, 493-497.

Sutherland, G. R. (1977). Fragile cites on human chromosomes, demonstration of their dependence on the type of tissue culture medium. *Science, 197*, 265-266.

Sutherland, G. R. (1982). Heritable fragile sites on human chromosomes. VIII. Preliminary population cytogenetics data on the folic-acid-sensitive fragile sites. *American Journal of Human Genetics, 34*, 452-458.

Sutherland, G. R., & Hecht, F. (1985). *Fragile sites on human chromosomes*. New York: Oxford University Press.

Suthers, G. K., Hyland, V. J., Callen, D. F., Oberlé, I., Rocchi, M., Thomas, N. S., Morris, C. P., Schwartz, G. E., Schmidt, M., Ropers, H. H., et al. (1991). Physical mapping of new DNA probes near the fragile X mutation (FRAXA) by using a panel of cell lines. *American Journal of Human Genetics, 47*, 187-195.

Thake, A., Todd, J., Webb, T., & Bundey, S. (1987). Children with the fragile X chromosome at schools for the mildly mentally retarded. *Developmental Medicine and Child Neurology, 29*, 711-719.

Tirosh, E., & Borochowitz, Z. (1992). Sleep apnea in fragile X syndrome. *American Journal of Medical Genetics, 43*, 124-127.

Towbin, K. E., Dykens, E. M., Pearson, G. S., & Cohen D. J. (1993). Conceptualizing "borderline syndrome of childhood" and "childhood schizophrenia" as a developmental disorder. *Journal of the American Academy of Child and Adolescent Psychiatry, 32*, 775-782.

Tranebjaerg, L., & Kure, P. (1991). Prevalence of fra(X) and other specific diagnoses in autistic individuals in a Danish county. *American Journal of Medical Genetics, 38*, 212-214.

Tranebjaerg, L., & Orum, A. (1991). Major depressive disorder as a prominent but underestimated feature of fragile X syndrome. *Comprehensive Psychiatry, 32*, 83-87.

Turner, G. (1983). Historical overview of X-linked mental retardation. In R. J. Hagerman & P. M. McBogg (Eds.), *The fragile X syndrome: Diagnosis, biochemistry, and intervention* (pp. 1-16). Dillon, CO: Spectra.

Turner, G., Brookwell, R., Daniel, A., Selikowitz, M., & Zilibowitz, M. (1980). Heterozygous expression of x-linked mental retardation and x-chromosome marker fra(x) (q27). *New England Journal of Medicine, 303*, 662-664.

Turner, G., Daniel, A., & Frost, M. (1980). X-linked mental retardation, macro-orchidism, and the Xq27 fragile site. *Journal of Pediatrics, 96*, 837-841.

Turner, G., Robinson, H., Laing, S., & Purvis-Smith, S. (1986). Preventative screening for the fragile X syndrome. *New England Journal of Medicine, 315*, 607-609.

Venter, P. A., Op'l Hof, J., Coezee, D. S., Van de Wa, H. C., & Retie, F. (1984). No marker X chromosome in autistic children. *Human Genetics, 67*, 107.

Verkerk, A. J., Pieretti, M., Sutcliffe, J. S., Fu, Y.-H., Kuhi, D. P., Pizzuti, A., Reiner, O., Richards, S., Victoria, M. F., Zhang, F., Eussen, B. E., van Ommen, G. J., Blonden,

L. A., Riggens, G. J., Chastain, J. L., Kunst, C. B., Galjaard, H., Caskey, C. T., Nelson, D. L., Oostra, B. A., & Warren, S. T. (1991). Identification of a gene (FMR-1) containing a CGG repeat coincident with a breakpoint cluster region exhibiting length variation in fragile X syndrome. *Cell, 65,* 905-914.

Vieregge, P., & Froster-Iskenius, U. (1989). Clinico-neurological investigations in the fragile X form of mental retardation. *Journal of Neurology, 236,* 85-92.

Vilkman, E., Niemi, J., & Ikonen, U. (1988). Fragile X speech phonology in Finnish. *Brain and Language, 34,* 203-221.

Volkmar, F. R. (1987). Social development. In D. J. Cohen, A. M. Donnellan, & R. Paul (Eds.), *Handbook of autism and pervasive developmental disorders* (pp. 41-60). New York: John Wiley.

Wahlstrom, J., Gillberg, C., Gustavson, K. H., & Holgren, G. (1986). Infantile autism and the fragile X: A Swedish multicenter study. *American Journal of Medical Genetics, 23,* 403-408.

Wahlstrom, J., Steffenburg, S., Helgren, L., & Gillberg, C. (1989). Chromosome findings in twins with early-onset autistic disorder. *American Journal of Medical Genetics, 32,* 19-21.

Warren, S. (1992, June). *Discovery of the FMR-1 gene.* Paper presented at the Third International Fragile X Conference, Snowmass Resort, CO.

Warren, S. T., Knight, S. J., Peters, J. F., Stayton, C. L., Consalez, G. G., Zhang, F. P., et al. (1990). Isolation of the human chromosomal band Xq28 within the somatic cell hybrids by fragile X site breakage. *Proceedings of the National Academy of Sciences USA, 87,* 3856-3860.

Watson, J. D. (1968). *The double helix.* New York: Mentor Books.

Watson, M. S., Breg, W. R., Pauls, D., Brown, W. T., Carroll, A. J., Howard-Peebles, P. N., Meryash, D., & Shapiro, L. R. (1988). Aneuploidy and the fragile X syndrome. *American Journal of Medical Genetics, 30,* 115-121.

Watson, M. S., Leckman, J. F., Annex, B., Breg, W. R., Boles, D., Volkmar, F. R., Cohen, D. J., & Carter, C. (1984). Fragile X in a survey of 75 autistic males. *New England Journal of Medicine, 301,* 1462.

Webb, T. (1989). The epidemiology of the fragile X syndrome. In K. E. Davies (Ed.), *The fragile X syndrome* (pp. 40-55). Oxford, UK: Oxford University Press.

Wechsler, D. (1981). *Wechsler Adult Intelligence Scale-Revised.* New York: Psychological Corporation.

Widaman, K. F., Borthwick-Duffy, S. A., & Little, T. D. (1991). The structure and development of adaptive behaviors. *International Review of Research in Mental Retardation, 17,* 1-54.

Wiegers, A. (1992, June). *Adaptive behavior in the fragile X syndrome.* Paper presented at the Third International Fragile X Conference, Snowmass Resort, CO.

Wikler, L., Wasow, M., & Hatfield, E. (1981). Chronic sorrow revisited: Parent vs. professional depiction of the adjustment of parents of mentally retarded children. *American Journal of Orthopsychiatry, 51,* 63-70.

Wilson, D. P., Carpenter, N. J., & Berkovitz, G. (1988). Thyroid function in men with fragile X-linked mental retardation. *American Journal of Medical Genetics, 31,* 733-734.

Wing, L. (1981). Asperger's syndrome: A clinical account. *Psychological Medicine, 11,* 115-129.

Wisniewski, K. E., Segan, S. M., Miezejeski, C. M., Sersen, E. A., & Rudelli, R. D. (1991). The fragile X syndrome: Neurological, electrophysiological, and neuropathological abnormalities. *American Journal of Medical Genetics, 38,* 476-480.

Wolff, P. H., Gardner, J., Lappen, J., Paccia, J., & Schnell, R. (1987, December). *Social adaptation and behavior in males with the fragile X syndrome.* Paper presented at the First National Fragile X Conference, Denver, CO.

Wolff, P. H., Gardner, J., Paccia, J., & Lappen, J. (1989). The greeting behavior of fragile X males. *American Journal on Mental Retardation, 93,* 406-411.

Wolf-Schein, E. G., Sudhalter, V., Cohen, I., Fisch, G. S., Hanson, D., Pfadt, A. G., Hagerman, R., Jenkins, E., & Brown, W. T. (1987). Speech-language and the fragile X syndrome: Initial findings. *Journal of the American Speech and Hearing Association (ASHA), 29,* 35-38.

Wright, H. H., Young, S. R., Edwards, J. G., Abramson, R. K., & Duncan, J. (1986). Fragile X syndrome in a population of autistic children. *Journal of the American Academy of Child and Adolescent Psychiatry, 25,* 641-644.

Yu, S., Pritchard, M. D., Kremer, E., Lynch, M., Nancarrow, J., Baker, E., Holman, K., Mulley, J. C., Warren, S. T., Schlessinger, D., Sutherland, G. R., & Richards, R. I. (1991). Fragile X genotype characterized by an unstable region of DNA. *Science, 252,* 1179-1181.

Zigler, E. (1967). Familial mental retardation: A continuing dilemma. *Science, 155,* 292-298.

Zigler, E., Balla, D., & Hodapp, R. (1984). On the definition and classification of mental retardation. *American Journal of Mental Deficiency, 89,* 215-230.

Zigler, E., & Hodapp, R. M. (1986a). How many retarded people are there? In E. Zigler & R. M. Hodapp, *Understanding mental retardation* (pp. 90-111). New York: Cambridge University Press.

Zigler, E., & Hodapp, R. M. (1986b). The retarded child as a whole person. In E. Zigler & R. M. Hodapp, *Understanding mental retardation* (pp. 115-135). New York: Cambridge University Press.

Zigler, E., & Hodapp, R. M. (1986c). The search for miracle cures. In E. Zigler & R. M. Hodapp, *Understanding mental retardation* (pp. 181-199). New York: Cambridge University Press.

AUTHOR INDEX

SUBJECT INDEX